YO-CCT-680

Fielding's
Moral Psychology

Fielding's
Moral Psychology

MORRIS GOLDEN

THE UNIVERSITY OF
MASSACHUSETTS PRESS
1966

Copyright © 1966
The University of Massachusetts Press
All rights reserved

Library of Congress Catalog Card Number 66-28115
Printed in the United States of America

*To Howard O. Brogan
and E. L. McAdam, Jr.
for what they have
taught me*

Preface

IN THE MIDST of Tom Jones's mounting troubles, he remained hopeful because he had a "sanguine temper," and, Fielding continues, "after having read much and considered long on that subject of happiness which hath employed so many great pens, I am almost inclined to fix it in the possession of this temper; which puts us, in a manner, out of the reach of Fortune, and makes us happy without her assistance" (XIII, vi). Such a statement, which suggests that happiness lies in disregarding the outside world and living within our own minds, brings Fielding soberly close to Swift's ironic definition of happiness as "a perpetual possession of being well deceived." Since happiness is a great positive good for Fielding (as it is not for Swift), perhaps the only achievable and valid earthly aim, his psychological ideal appears to be the mind serenely protected against the world.

If this were Fielding's total view of man's condition, he would be merely an anomaly in the vigorous eighteenth century, a bittersweet recorder of the victories of men who cannot cope with an incomprehensible world—men like Huxley's Sir Hercules, the midget who commits a classical suicide when confronted with the normal hugeness and indelicacy of his son. In more violent moods, he might have glorified lonely titans like Manfred or Jake Barnes or Birkin without his Ursula.

Such aloofness, however, would be not only anachronistic but largely antipathetic to the personality which Lady Mary Wortley Montagu magnificently eulogized in a letter to her daughter: "I am sorry for H. Fielding's death, not only as I shall read no more of his writings, but I believe he lost more than others, as no man enjoyed life more than he did. . . . His happy constitution (even when he had, with great pains, half demolished it) made him forget every thing when he was before a venison pasty, or over a flask of champagne, and I am persuaded he has known more happy moments than any prince upon earth . . . . [he] was so formed for happiness, it is pity he was not immortal." Such a personality was lost without society, as Fielding well knew. In a cheerful interlude in the pains of his last illness, he wrote, "I was left in a disposition of enjoying an agreeable hour, without the assistance of a companion, which has always appeared to me necessary to such enjoyment. . . ." The only waking adult on the ship to Lisbon was the captain; and with him, despite his ignorance, pride, insensitivity, and deafness, Fielding sat down to a bowl of punch.

Fielding was insatiably concerned with social relations, and he therefore could not be contented with a vision of man as proudly or maniacally isolated from his fellows. No more than Tom could he deny the existence of companions, or venison, or the walls of a prison. Like Locke, and like most of his own contemporaries, he wanted to synthesize, not repudiate. In his essays, he tended to emphasize one or the other aspect of man's existence—the isolation or the obligations in a material and social world. But in the novels, he insisted that complexity and paradox are basic to any honest portrayal of the relations between the self and the surrounding world. Through the nature and actions of his creatures, Fielding asserted the difficulty and yet the necessity of reconciling a psychology of self-contained happiness, a philosophy that accepts the existence of the material world, and a moral theory that demands excursive love. These are the elements of Fielding's vision of man in society and, therefore, the materials of which his novels were made.

In the following study, I shall try to describe Fielding's theory of psychology and its connection with his view of morality. To this end, I shall first examine his formulations in the relatively abstract and tentative miscellaneous writings and then try to show how, in the novels, he applied them to an ambitious imitation of human life. Where I discuss the moral and psychological views of Fielding's contemporaries, near-contemporaries, and classical predecessors, I am not concerned to be exhaustive, or even to show precise influence. Rather, I wish to establish an intellectual context for Fielding's ideas and representations, which are the subject of this book.

I had hoped to study Fielding's thought extensively, but I

found myself anticipated by so many illuminating works that I have settled for a small slice of it. Unlike Tristram Shandy, I undertook a folio, but matter shrank under my hand. The footnotes will indicate the range and depth of my indebtedness, but I must mention here that without the superb discussions of Fielding's thought and manner by Martin C. Battestin, Alan D. Mc-Killop, Henry K. Miller, George Sherburn, Ian Watt, and James A. Work, even such an octavo as the following could scarcely have made sense. It is also a pleasure to record my gratitude for their kindness to the library staffs of Amherst College, Mount Holyoke College, Smith College, Yale University, and the University of Massachusetts. And I am deeply grateful to Professors Battestin and Miller and to my colleagues Professors Richard Haven and John C. Weston, Jr., for their kind and careful reading of my manuscript and their valuable suggestions for revision.

Contents

Abbreviations

WHILE WE WAIT for the new edition of Fielding's writings which is soon to flow from the Wesleyan University Press, we must gather our texts where we can. All references to the novels will consist of book and chapter numbers, so that readers who do not have access to Henley's edition of the *Works* or to Mr. Battestin's of *Joseph Andrews* will not be inconvenienced.

Works   *The Complete Works of Henry Fielding, Esq.*, ed. W. E. Henley (New York: Croscup and Sterling, 1902), 16 Vols.

JA&S   *Joseph Andrews* and *Shamela*, ed. Martin C. Battestin (Boston: Houghton Mifflin, 1961). Riverside ed.

CGJ   *The Covent-Garden Journal*, ed. Gerard Edward Jensen (New Haven: Yale University Press, 1915), 2 Vols.

Journal   *The Journal of a Voyage to Lisbon*, ed. Harold E. Pagliaro (New York: Nardon Press, 1963).

Fielding's
Moral Psychology

I

The Enclosed Self

THOUGH THE CONFRONTATION of man's egocentric mind and an ambiguous world has been perennially unsettling (as King Lear, Raskolnikov, and most twentieth-century heroes would testify), it seems to have been more disturbing in the eighteenth century than at other times before our own. Relatively few writers went so far as Berkeley in questioning the existence of matter; but a great many, among them Locke and his followers, were uncertain that one could know what it was. At opposite ends of the century, it is true, were opposite poles of certainty in Swift and Blake. The progress of epistemology among literary men—if progress is the word—was from Swift's straightforward assumption that a real and knowable world exists outside man and that it is man's duty, if he is to be sane, useful, and pious, to know this reality, to Blake's view that the only reality is the human imagination. Any argument that the changes were simply chronological would be foolish, easily refuted by Johnson's famous refutation of Berkeley nine years after Fielding's death; nevertheless, it seems generally true that writers between Swift and Blake leaned toward various forms of sentimentalism, or sympathy, or the doctrine of feeling, all connected through the idea of the sympathetic imagination: the belief that man could understand other things and people, and perhaps communicate with them, through learning to feel what they felt. Hence the emphasis everywhere on feeling—in Collins' evocation of the imagined effects of his collections of passions, in Thomson's global rendition of the miseries of winter, in Sterne's exploration of the sensibilities of an ass, and so on. Fielding, always concerned with showing humanity how to act rightly, faced the same problem of understanding man's psychological and moral condition, and used orthodox methods of trying to solve it. Examining his efforts to resolve the paradox of an enclosed mind which yet must establish outgoing sympathy may therefore clarify both important elements in his art and some of the central moral positions of his time.

For a basic question—how is man to act in the world?—a variety of answers was available in the contemporary store of ideas. One, of great prominence in Fielding's thinking, is in the classical inheritance, particularly the ethical systems of Aristotle, Plato, and the stoics (among whom he frequently cites Cicero and Seneca). All three assert the existence of moral absolutes; but Aristotle's influence is dominant in the direction of demanding such moral actions as those of the wayfaring Abraham Adams, Joseph Andrews, and Tom Jones, who move out of themselves to participate in the lives of others. Plato and the stoics, to continue this simplification, argue that the good man can be impervious to outer circumstances, deriving his happiness from within himself. Orthodox Christian thinkers approved both avenues, insisting only that the inner satisfaction and the outside action must be supported and guaranteed by religious faith. More recently, Descartes' analysis, centering all knowable reality in the mind, had inevitably called into question the possibility of moral action.

The epistemology of John Locke, influenced by Descartes and dominant in the period, begins with the mind's unfortunate self-enclosure and its need to know the outside world. As Fielding and his contemporaries knew, Locke believed that the mind can perceive two sets of ideas. The first of these is sensation, contributed by the senses; the second, reflection, is "the perception of the operations of our own mind within us, as it is employed about the ideas it has got; which operations when the soul comes to reflect on and consider, do furnish the understanding with another set of ideas, which could not be had from things without. . . . This source of ideas every man has wholly in himself. . . ."[1] Locke here seems to be relating the outer world and the inner, but he soon shows that we cannot know the outer world with certainty: such "sensible qualities" as taste, smell, color, sound, "whatever reality we by mistake attribute to them, are in truth nothing in the objects themselves, but powers to produce various sensations in us . . ." (II, viii, 14). It follows, that of these ideas of secondary qualities, "There is nothing like our ideas existing in the bodies themselves. They are in the bodies, we denominate from them, only a power to produce those sensations in us; and what is sweet, blue, or warm in idea, is but the certain bulk, figure, and motion of the insensible parts in the bodies themselves, which we call so" (II, viii, 15). Since no man can know the nature of the outside world, or the mind of another, different people will attach different meanings to the same words. For communication, which is essential to man, Locke therefore advised the use of the most precise words possible, but he concluded that unless the two minds are attuned in the same direction—are in sympathy—even approximate understanding is very hard to achieve.[2]

In his moral deductions, Locke stayed rigorously within the implications of his secular epistemology: "Pleasure and pain, and that which causes them, good and evil, are the hinges on which our passions turn . . ." (II, xx, 3); "hatred or love, to beings capable of happiness or misery, is often the uneasiness or delight which we find in ourselves, arising from a consideration of their very being or happiness. Thus the being and welfare of a man's children or friends, producing constant delight in him, he is said constantly to love them. But it suffices to note, that our ideas of love and hatred are but the dispositions of the mind, in respect of pleasure and pain in general, however caused in us" (II, xx, 5). So much can be deduced from our knowledge of man as a thinking animal; with his divine soul Locke cannot meddle. All our moral views—except those revealed by Christianity—have their sources purely in our internal desires for comfort.

Two major complexes of thought on man's moral nature, consistent with Locke's epistemology but diametrically opposed to each other, fought for dominance through the century. Fielding vacillated between them, sometimes accepting both in the same paragraph. In essence, one held that man was bad, the other that he was good. The religiously dominant puritans of the seventeenth century had insisted on the pre-eminence of grace as the only counter to man's innate depravity, and Hobbes had powerfully supported this assumption, seeing man as dominated by selfishness. Both offered the conclusion that man needed to exert his will or develop appropriate social machinery to repress the dangerous passions, which reason was unable to curb and which indeed made of reason a helpless tool.

In response, the latitudinarian divines of the late seventeenth and eighteenth centuries, whom Fielding frequently quoted with approval, argued that man was benevolent.[3] In a significant essay, R. S. Crane has sketched the views that united them, of which the following are most relevant to Fielding. To the classical influence supporting self-enclosed detachment, Crane shows, these divines opposed "what they insisted was the true Christian idea of a charity which derives both its force and value from the fact that the good man does permit himself to be 'inwardly disturbed.' "[4] They argued that man's heart is " 'naturally' good in the sense that when left to its own native impulses it tends invariably to humane and sociable feelings . . ." (p. 220). They proposed "Self-approving Joy" as the good man's reward and frequently repeated "how enjoyable the benevolent emotions may be to the individual who allows himself to feel them" (p. 227). However, they did not go so far as Fielding into the paradoxical position that mental pleasure is the *only* earthly reward for outer action.

Hobbes's eighteenth-century follower, Mandeville, insisted that in contemporary life one can see evidence only for an opposite view of human nature. All human actions, he maintained, derive from self-love and pride or vanity: "The vast Esteem we have of ourselves, and the small Value we have for others, makes us all very unfair Judges in our own Cases."[5] Even well-bred gentlemen, to say nothing of the vulgar, are ignorant of their own motives and habitually avoid introspection lest they discover unpleasant truths. For the well-bred man, "enquiring within, and boldly searching into one's own Bosom, must be the most shocking Employment, that a Man can give his Mind to, whose greatest Pleasure consists in secretly admiring himself" (II, 80). Essentially, Mandeville anticipated Freud in seeing man as motivated by the undisciplined, ignoble needs of the self as the unconscious perceives them. More directly to our purpose, he also furnished one aspect of Fielding's appraisal of mankind. Whenever Fielding exposed evil in man or society—whenever he was most "realistic"—he relied on such a reduction as Mandeville's.

Mandeville's chief secular opponent, Shaftesbury—whom Fielding frequently cited respectfully—aimed for a conscious and rational assertion of moral goodness, on the basis often of an epistemology which makes sympathy the path toward knowledge. In his *Characteristicks* he insisted that internal virtue leads in a socially useful direction; indeed, the moral sense depends on an awareness of the likely responses of others.[6] In this connection, Shaftesbury also argued that good and evil are selfishly determined, since all rational creatures must be aware that if they voluntarily hurt anyone, others will fear and mistrust them. Such knowledge is the sense of right and wrong. People like Hobbes, he wrote, claim that a wise creature consults only its own good, not society's, but the truth is "That to be well affected towards the *Publick Interest* and *one's own,* is not only consistent, but inseparable: and that moral rectitude, or *Virtue,* must accordingly be the Advantage, and *Vice* the Injury and Disadvantage of every Creature" (II, 81). Virtue of this sort seems to start in social awareness and end in social action: natural affection, the central social virtue, is the "master passion." Another natural pleasure, derived from scientific knowledge, is the joy of contemplating the harmony of the world. And even superior and more pleasant is *"virtuous Motion,* and *the Exercise of Benignity and Goodness"* (II, 105).

Furthermore, this outward action ultimately leads to inward comfort: "And as in the case of *Partiality,* or vitious Friendship, which has no rule or order, every Reflection of the Mind necessarily makes to its disadvantage, and lessens the Enjoyment; so in the case of *Integrity,* the Consciousness of just Behaviour towards Mankind in general, casts a good reflection on each friendly Affection in particular, and raises the Enjoyment of Friendship still the higher, in the way of *Community* or *Participation* above-mention'd" (II, 111-112). The pleasures themselves "are wholly founded in *An easy Temper, free of Harshness, Bitterness, or Distaste;* and in *A Mind or Reason well compos'd, quiet, easy within itself, and such as can freely bear its own Inspection and Review"* (II, 114). Since the chief pleasures are mental, he goes on, echoing Plato, and since they derive from the natural affections, "it follows, That *to have the natural Affections, is to have the chief Means and Power of Self-Enjoyment, the highest Possession and Happiness of Life"* (II, 126). Therefore, the ultimate criterion of virtue is mental pleasure.

Fixing desire on outward things leads to great unhappiness if they are unobtainable or removed; one must place value "in *the Affections* or *Sentiments,* in the *governing Part* and *inward Character;* we have then the full Enjoyment of it within our power: The *Imagination* or *Opinion* remains steddy and irreversible:

And the *Love, Desire* and *Appetite* is answer'd; without Apprehension of Loss or Disappointment" (II, 198).[7] Man derives his sense of satisfaction from pursuing the good of his society, from being in harmony with the harmony of the world.

Whether the injunction to get out of the self and act benevolently derives from Aristotle or from contemporary liberal theologians, whether the persuasion of enclosure is a consequence of Fielding's reading of Shaftesbury or of Locke cannot certainly be determined; but there was clearly a good deal of precedent, both ancient and contemporary, for such views. In his essays, which are usually concerned with separate moral or social issues, he is likely to follow one stream of thought or another. But in his novels he roams eclectically through his intellectual interests, since he is examining not only theoretical man but actual men within the diverse, unsystematic society of eighteenth-century England. Attempts to fit him completely or even predominantly in one tradition cannot be wholly successful. In one of the best recent studies of Fielding, for example, Martin Battestin places Fielding mainly in the optimistic camp of the liberal churchmen, persuaded that any man can be saved if he but wills to be good, that any man has the elements of goodness in him.[8] Yet on this very issue, it is often demonstrable that Fielding, seeing men as enclosed within minds that have been determined by innate dispositions and by environment, leans away from the churchmen toward the Hobbesian and classical tradition and finds very little chance of change once the mold has set. It has been argued that there is such a change in Tom Jones, a turn toward prudence after his glimpse of the horrors to which wildness might lead; but Tom has not been very wild, he is young and in the process of maturing, and he is lured toward virtue by a summit of felicity which can beckon few others. Booth, despite Fielding's provision of Barrow's sermons, is saved by events and by his agreement to stay away from London, not by a flowering of good sense. The ultimate criterion of a satisfactory life for Fielding is happiness, which he sees as the psychological consequence of innate disposition interacting with society, a view for which he had no one source.

In the dramatic and miscellaneous writings from the beginning to the end of Fielding's career, he is regularly concerned with how human nature is affected by the conflicting calls of outer action and inward peace. What seem to be individual commonplaces form a lifelong pattern of consistent and vigorous thought. His first play, *Love in Several Masques,* already indicates his concern with self-enclosure and sympathetic association; only the possession of certain virtues can allow one to perceive them in others. Merital, the most attractive figure in the play, says that "women are like books. Malice and envy will easily lead you to the detection of their faults; but their beauties good judgment only can discover and good nature relish" (*Works,* VIII, 29). In *The Coffee-House Politician* (1730) Fielding applies this psychological approach to the audience in his Prologue:

> And while these scenes the conscious knave displease,
> Who feels within the criminal he sees,
> The uncorrupt and good must smile, to find
> No mark for satire in his generous mind. (*Works,* IX, 76)

During the play itself the vicious Justice Squeezum, like the morally diseased political lord in *Amelia,* at the end of Fielding's career, unconsciously sees the world as a reflection of himself: "I am sorry the age is so corrupt. Really I expect to see some grievous and heavy judgment fall on the nation. We are as bad as ever Sodom and Gomorrah were; and I wish we may not be as miserable" (*Works,* IX, 102).

Another play, *The Universal Gallant* (1735), touches on the idea of delusion, which is inescapably connected with self-enclosure. Mondish says of Col. Raffler that he delightedly thinks his wife constant: "And that is the same as if she were so in reality; for, if a man be happy in his own opinion, I see little reason why he should trouble himself about the world's" (*Works,* XI, 93). There is irony in this commonplace, but it assumes theories about the nature of happiness and the machinery of knowledge which become important and relatively fresh in Fielding's later performances. The concluding couplet of this play reaffirms the tie between the mind and the world:

The jealous their own miseries create,
And make themselves the very thing they hate. (*Works,* XI, 160)

To anticipate chronologically, in Fielding's posthumously performed play, *The Fathers,* he insists on self-approving joy as the only certain reward in a world that is often malicious, but he nonetheless shows that virtue may well prosper through its operation on others. Boncour, the hero, argues that virtue must go out of the self into action in the world: "How wretched is that animal, whose whole happiness centres in himself; who cannot feel any satisfaction, but in the indulgence of his own appetite" (*Works,* XII, 166). After rumors of his impoverishment, and the consequent ingratitude of his beneficiaries, are supposed to show him the worthlessness of his goodness, he refuses to be daunted: "Why should I be sorry that I have been good, because others are evil? If I have acted right I have done well, though alone; if wrong, the sanction of all mankind would not justify my conduct" (*Works,* XII, 210).

The sympathetic association or inference is coupled with virtuous hedonism in the preface to the *Miscellanies,* where Fielding professes not to understand why men go to so much trouble to be villains when being decent is so clear and easy: "Nor hath goodness less advantage in the article of pleasure than of honour over this kind of greatness. The same righteous judge always annexes a bitter anxiety to the purchases of guilt, whilst it adds a double sweetness to the enjoyments of innocence and virtue: for fear, which all the wise agree is the most wretched of human evils, is, in some degree, always attending on the former, and never can in any manner molest the happiness of the latter" (*Works,* XII, 244). The combination of greatness and goodness, he says in a startlingly relevant image, is "the true sublime in human nature. That elevation by which the soul of man, raising and extending itself above the order of this creation, and brightened with a certain ray of divinity, looks down on the condition of mortals" (*Works,* XII, 245). Like the soul which Shelley addresses in *Adonais,* or like Cicero's stoic ideal, the good man's soul partakes of the divine as it watches sympathetically, but above the strife. Nowhere else does Fielding so strongly suggest that the arena of action—eighteenth-century English society—is no more than a testing ground for the mind.

The "Essay on Conversation," which appeared in the *Miscellanies,* elaborates on the idea of social conventions as devices for educating people to a feeling for others, to getting out of selfish concerns. Here, following Shaftesbury and Aristotle, Fielding says that man is a social animal: "rejectors of society borrow all their information from their own savage dispositions" (*Works,* XIV, 245), rather than learn it from life around them. The central rule of good breeding is also the central rule of morality; but its application requires solving one of the more serious problems confronting human happiness: "*Do unto all men as you would they should do unto you* . . . whoever is well read in the book of nature, and hath made much observation on the actions of men, will perceive so few capable of judging, or rightly pursuing their own happiness, that he will be apt to conclude, that some attention is necessary . . . to enable men to know truly, *what they would have done unto them,* or, at least, what it would be their interest to *have done*" (*Works,* XIV, 249). The worst offenders against society, in such a view, are "insolence or haughtiness," since they give man a pride in himself coupled with contempt for the rest of humanity, and "this contempt of others is the truest symptom of a base and a bad heart" (*Works,* XIV, 263).[9] A cause of delusion, disdain prevents its subject from knowing himself or the outside world; in denying the equal humanity of others, it prevents virtuous action and consequent mental peace.

The most notable work in the *Miscellanies, Jonathan Wild,* is directly concerned with a paragon of selfishness, a model of complete inability to consider others as human. Selfishness—impregnable enclosure within the self—is the essence of the false "greatness" which the book is designed to expose. Great men like Wild —Plato's tyrant with Machiavellian trimmings—measure their success by the magnitude of the ruin they can spread. Seeking power only for the pride it can feed, they are as miserable as their subjects materially, and more miserable psychologically.

Heartfree, by contrast, was happy in seeing the world as a reflection of his own innocence: he "was of an honest and open disposition. He was of that sort of men whom experience only, and not their own natures, must inform that there are such things as deceit and hypocrisy in the world" (II, i). By reflecting on religion, Heartfree "worked himself up into an enthusiasm which by degrees soon became invulnerable to every human attack" (III, ii). Wild, of course, distrusted Heartfree: Wild, "not being able on the strictest examination to find in a certain spot of human nature called his own heart the least grain of that pitiful low quality called honesty, had resolved, perhaps a little too generally, that there was no such thing" (III, x). In each case, the character can see outside him only the qualities within himself, a situation immediately dangerous to the virtuous innocent, but ultimately worse for the monster.

In the development of the novel, the downfall of Wild and his various low-lived confederates is perfectly plausible—indeed, Fielding had the actual career of Wild as a guide, as well as the short biographies by Defoe and others. But the saving of Heartfree is occasioned by pure good fortune, as the ironic narrator makes clear. As early as *Jonathan Wild* Fielding faced the problem of not really believing that virtue and piety, unsupported by prudence (which, despite classical tradition, he saw as probably inconsistent with them), could safely live in the world. It even appears at times that for Fielding *no* character can be both sufficiently self-enclosed and sufficiently outgoing to assure any sort of triumph over the combination of evil in society and the tricks played by time and chance.

As *Jonathan Wild* suggests, Fielding relies on fantasies, on the techniques of the romance, for happy endings, while destruction needs no more than the realistic working out of the inevitabilities of character. Except for the "great and good," the ideals of the Preface to the *Miscellanies,* the mind's imperviousness to reality almost necessarily leads to defeat. Theoretically, the worthy person must acquire an awareness of evil through experience, since he has almost none of it within; he can easily enough recognize good, which is his own reflection. This argument, in Fielding's preface to his sister's *David Simple* (1744), explains what he considers her remarkable perceptiveness: "a very little knowledge of the world will afford an observer, moderately accurate, sufficient instances of evil; and a short communication with her own heart, will leave the author of this book very little to seek abroad of all the good which is to be found in human nature" (*Works*, XVI, 13). But in his fiction, where he assumes the responsibility of showing full human nature at work in society, he is no more hopeful than Johnson's Nekayah, who explains that marrying old is bad, marrying young is bad, expecting to seize an optimum middle time for marrying is chimerical, and not marrying is worst of all. Prudence, Fielding's middle ground on which the good mind can meet reality, never seems available to the virtuous until authorial fantasy—"romance"—has provided them with permanent felicity.

Fielding's journal leaders, like his plays, verse, and miscellaneous essays, frequently return to the basic problem of reconciling outgoing virtue with the fact of inward reward or punishment. In *The Champion*, for example, Fielding several times asserts the connection between virtue and communication and between the inward sense and the perception of the outer world. An early issue (December 11, 1739) argues that

Those authors, who have set human nature in a very vile and detestable light, however right or wrong such their sentiments may be or whatever success they may have met with in the world, have often succeeded in establishing an infamous character to themselves; for, though they observe with the utmost accuracy, the outward behaviour of others, they will seldom be able to draw any inferences which can lead them to the springs or causes of those actions; they must therefore receive all their information from within. At least, those who deduce actions, apparently good, from evil causes, can trace them only through the windings of their own hearts; and while they attempt to draw an ugly picture of human nature, they must of necessity copy the deformity from their own minds. (*Works*, XV, 94)

He continues that though the existence of hypocrites may make us cautious, this is no proof, except to a corrupt mind, of human depravity.

For a time in *The Champion* Fielding is especially interested in Locke's theory of communication, particularly as it relates to moral judgments. In the issue of January 17, 1740, he cites Locke on the emptiness of the sounds that usually pass from speaker to hearer. Two weeks later he is worried about the possibility of bad communication with ourselves: "It hath been observed, that we often mistake the actions of others, as good or evil, from not knowing the springs whence those actions proceed: but what if we are as great strangers to the springs of even our own actions!" (*Works*, XV, 179). Pride, he says, is likely to be the chief cause of misunderstanding; not only is the self liable to enclosed isolation, but parts of it may be actively concerned to isolate and delude other parts.

A pair of essays directly ties good nature, Fielding's chief source of virtue, to Locke's epistemology. One, in *The Champion* of March 27, 1740, discusses the current argument about the meaning of goodness, which Fielding says arose because of semantic confusion: "I am apt to suspect, when I see sensible men totally differ in opinion concerning any general word, that the complex idea in their several minds which this word represents is compounded of very different simples" (*Works*, XV, 257). In support he cites Locke on the confusion caused by the different understanding of words, and provides a specific definition of the sort demanded by the philosopher: "Good-nature is a delight in the happiness of mankind, and a concern at their misery, with a desire, as much as possible to procure the former, and avert the latter. . . . It is not that cowardice which prevents us from repelling or resenting an injury; for it doth not divest us of humanity, and like charity, though it doth not end, may at least begin at home" (*Works*, XV, 258). Considering good nature here as a passion, he points out that it is capable of limitless satisfaction, as the other passions are not. It is thus the best possible quality, motivating continued excursions into the world and offering matchless internal rewards to the mind.

For the same reasons, good nature is the supremely humanizing quality, the divine gift that can alone quiet Fielding's basic fear of complete self-enclosure, a fear which envisions the disintegration of society, as he suggests in *The True Patriot* (No. 23):

I have heard of a man who believed there was no real existence in the world but himself; and that whatever he saw without him was mere phantom and illusion. . . . This philosopher, I imagine, hath not had many followers in theory; and yet if we were to derive the principles of mankind from their practice, we should be almost persuaded that somewhat like this madness had possessed not only particular men, but their several orders and professions. For though they do not absolutely deny all existence to other persons and things, yet it is certain they hold them of no consequence, and little worth their consideration, unless they trench somewhat towards their own order or calling. (*Works*, XIV, 50)

Various professions or social classes, he says, read books and respond to plays along the lines of their own limitations. In public life, also, people are unable to see outside their own opinions and supposed interests and in consequence cause great confusion and danger. Though Fielding cannot help responding to the self-enclosed implication of Locke's philosophy, he attaches himself, sometimes desperately, to good nature as the cure.

The Covent-Garden Journal reveals a generally similar view of morality, though the later Fielding is more alert to the evil in man than to the good. While the constitution of human nature and the definitions of good and evil remain the same to him throughout his career, in his writings of the 1750's—*Amelia*, the *Journal of a Voyage to Lisbon, The Covent-Garden Journal, A Proposal for . . . Provision for the Poor*—he is more depressed by what he sees than he had been earlier. In an essay on the evil of slanderous and scurrilous writing, for example, he says that slander is not to be excused by the disavowal of malice: "For if we have no Malice, we are the less likely to have received any Provocation; and our Cruelty is to be imputed only to that Malignity which is the rankest and most poisonous Weed that disgraces human Nature" (*CGJ*, I, 221). The writers of slander and scurrility may be slightly excused by poverty, but he does not see how to excuse the reader, whose interest must derive from "those Bogs of human Nature whence such a depraved Taste can arise" (*CGJ*, I, 223). More generally, "In the worthiest human Minds, there are some small innate Seeds of Malignity, which it is greatly in our Power either to suffocate and suppress, or to forward and improve their Growth, 'till they blossom and bear their poisonous Fruit; for which execrable Purpose, there is no Manure so effectual as those of Scandal, Scurrility, and Abuse" (*CGJ*, I, 232). The seeds are presumably the same as those which Fielding had noted early in his career, but to the weary police magistrate, a corrupt society seemed far readier to nurture them than he had believed likely.

In the plays as well as in the novels which follow, a major aspect of the central paradoxical theme of outward action and inward reward is a great concern for reputation, society's response to the appearance of men's moral actions. Hypocrisy is a cardinal sin for Fielding because he is deeply concerned for the relations between the mind and the reality outside it. General acclaim is due the virtuous man, because his mind is so disposed as to motivate his actions only for the good of society. He can be pleased only if he acts virtuously. But because of the ambiguity inherent in attempts to communicate, his good will may not be evident. The hypocrite, corrupting communication, may be responsible for others' confusion about reality and therefore about the direction in which virtuous action is to go.

Reputation is a recurrent issue in the plays, most conspicuously in *The Modern Husband*, that bitter early study of the most sordid elements in *Amelia*. Mr. Modern, who has lived by occasionally selling his wife, upbraids her temporary caution: "Very strange! that a woman who made so little scruple of sacrificing the substance of her virtue, should make so much of parting with the shadow of it." Mrs. Modern, equally vicious, answers that " 'Tis the shadow only that is valuable—Reputation is the soul of virtue" (Works, X, 17). In *The Universal Gallant* the point is made in somewhat more detail. The whorish Mrs. Raffler tells her sister-in-law Lady Raffler, "Take my word for it, child, pure nature won't do, the world will easily see your faults, but your virtues must be shown artfully, or they will not be discovered. Art goes beyond nature; and a woman who has only virtue in her face will pass much better through the world than she who has it only in her heart" (Works, XI, 96).[10] The "world," evidently, has an unfortunate tendency to misjudge, to think the worst of all motives, because the world is made up of people like the Man of the Hill, whose innocence has been destroyed by the discovery of falsehood. Only the internal sense of rectitude—derivable from good nature, which the world cannot see—can give consolation and peace. We are back in the mind, in this case a refuge for the outgoing self which has been misjudged.

The problem of discovering and understanding deceit, which is dramatized in *Jonathan Wild,* forms the subject of another piece in the *Miscellanies,* the "Essay on the Knowledge of the Characters of Men." Some people, Fielding says, seem to be born with deceit, which "is nourished and improved by education, in which we are taught rather to conceal vices than to cultivate virtues" and by lessons "in the Art of thriving." Unlike the stoic ideal of service to society, such an education in practicality "points out to every individual his own particular and separate advantage, to which he is to sacrifice the interest of all others" (Works, XIV, 282). He is not a man, a social animal, but a selfish force promoting chaos: "Thus while the crafty and designing part of mankind, consulting only their own separate advantage, endeavour to maintain one constant imposition on others, the whole world becomes a vast masquerade, where the greatest part appear disguised under false vizors and habits; a very few only showing their own faces, who become by so doing, the astonishment and ridicule of all the rest" (Works, XIV, 283).

Reputation, therefore, is often a misleading guide for the well-disposed man seeking to know the world: "Nor is there any more simple, unjust, and insufficient method of judging mankind, than by public estimation, which is oftener acquired by deceit, partiality, prejudice, and such like, than by real desert" (*Works*, XIV, 290). The hypocrite lives in steady fear of discovery, sympathetic to all of society's suspiciousness, "And thus, as nothing hates more violently than fear, many an innocent person, who suspects no evil intended him, is detested by him who intends it" (*Works*, XIV, 296). Like Hume, and like Locke before him, Fielding insists that the best test of character is to observe men's actions with others, especially with those closely connected to them. We cannot be sure of appearances, and we cannot trust words. Actions are also ambiguous. But if we can learn enough of another's circumstances, or at least build up a knowledge of enough of his actions, a meaningful pattern may emerge, and we can judge him.

At about the same time,[11] Fielding continued to examine hypocrisy and reputation in some of the leaders which he was writing for *The Champion*. In one (January 15, 1740) he argued that long-maintained reputation is usually deserved: "By authority, then, I understand, that weight which one man bears in the mind of another, resulting from an opinion of any extraordinary qualities or virtues inherent in him, which prepares the latter to receive the most favourable impression from all the words and actions of the person thus esteemed: this opinion, when it becomes general of any man, constitutes what we call popularity, which whoever hath attained, may with great facility procure any thing which it is in the power of the people to confer on him, may persuade them to, or dissuade them from any purposes" (*Works*, XV, 153). Similarly, people widely thought ill of can achieve nothing with the public, and this "universal ill opinion" is usually merited.

Two months later, however, in the issue for March 4, 1740, we find him writing that "There can be nothing so discouraging from the pursuit of reputation as a reflection, which we too often see occasion to make, that it is the prize of the undeserving" (*Works*, XV, 227) and that good men may not think it worth seeking. A major reason is that

True virtue is of a retired and quiet nature, content with herself, not at all busied in courting the acclamations of the crowd; she is plain and sober in her habit, sure of her innate worth, and therefore neglects to adorn herself with those gaudy colours, which catch the eyes of the giddy multitude. Vice, on the contrary, is of a noisy and boisterous disposition, despising herself, and jealous of the contempt of others, always meditating how she may acquire the applause of the world, gay and fluttering in her appearance, certain of her own ill features, and therefore careful by all the tricks of art to impose on and engage the affections of her beholders. (*Works*, XV, 228)

The meritorious man, aware of his own deserts, disdains practicing the tricks necessary for praise. As often, Fielding is concerned with a worthy ideal—Authority as the source of Reputation—which becomes corrupted, by selfishness acting through false appearances, into Hypocrisy as the source of Reputation. Failing widespread reform, the only consolations lie in weighing the temporary against the permanent and in the assurance of internal rewards. Though the bad man may earn a good reputation, he is always uneasy lest he be found out, and it never outlives him. A good man, however, can be secure in his reputation, which will survive him; if he does not gain such a reputation, he can see in this very lack an argument for the certainty of a future state, since a just God must reward virtue.

For the period, then, and for Fielding, a central problem of epistemology as it affected moral behavior was the need to perceive, and to act in, the outside world and the great difficulty of doing so. Those, like Shaftesbury, who believed in the goodness of human nature, generally argued that getting out of the self to do charitable actions is the essence of goodness, for which the reward is an internal sense of contentment and harmony. Those, like Mandeville, who saw human nature as selfish, thought that only saintly self-denial can be the fruit of virtuous motivation, but that the requirements of social living can channel this selfishness usefully.

Moral rules, Locke shows, are no more innate than any others, as can be seen from men's actions, not their professions. The implication for Fielding's thought is clear: on short acquaintance one can uncertainly deduce motivation from actions; after observing and considering many actions, one has a good idea of the essence of the character and can estimate the motivation properly, even when the action seems inappropriate. To anticipate, Allworthy's treatment of Jenny Jones, Partridge, and Tom is kindly in motivation, its apparent severity resulting from distorted information which renders their behavior abhorrent to a good nature; the landlady's corruption by Northerton's looks and money is deducible from her freeing him, despite her protestations to the contrary. For Locke, all our moral views except those revealed by Christianity have their source in our internal desire for comfort, for pleasure over pain. Shaftesbury, interested in proving man's nobility, finds virtue and contentment in the individual to consist largely in his sympathy with the good of the species. The ultimate secular criterion of virtue, in either case, is the mental pain or pleasure of the individual. The landlady, preferring immediate selfish pleasure to the serenity which rewards the well-adjusted social man, will always be the prey of her desires. Allworthy, chastising evil even against his own immediate urge toward kindliness, will always derive satisfaction from an awareness that he acts for the common good.

From the beginning of his writing career, Fielding sees the aim and reward of the good life as happiness, a purely psychological condition consequent on one's awareness of one's own benevolence, on a Shaftesburian harmony with one's kind. But harmony with one's kind requires a wide-ranging awareness of, and responsiveness to, its variety; and yet happiness is lodged within the mind. In an effort to resolve part of this enduring paradox, Fielding argues that the mind must send emissaries to external reality and rove among other human beings, but that it can naturally recognize only those moral qualities in man and society that correspond to what is within itself. On the question of whether, through experience, the mind can develop an intellectual awareness of what is not within it, Fielding vacillates. He is eager for the achievement of such awareness, attempts to teach it in all his writings, but can be certain of no mechanism capable of providing it. Weak or inexperienced good men, like Heartfree, respond only to virtuous signals, with which they are in sympathy, and so they can easily be made victims. Fielding's sad tendency, from the beginning of his career as a writer of fiction, is to see his function as that of providing elements of romance to prevent the reality of contemporary life from destroying the good.

With pain and pleasure our only stimuli and our only rewards, it seems at first inexplicable that some people still engage in violent evil, disturbing others and themselves. The cause, Fielding suggests, is a misreading of the signals—the assumption that "greatness" really means prestige in the world—coupled with a self-enclosed refusal to grant humanity to others. Essentially, it is the substitution of competition for sympathy and self-approval. As punishment, the evil, like Jonathan Wild, live within their own delusive creation, a permanent hell of selfish competition. Unable to defer any gratification, self-enclosed evil men aggressively attack society, from which they tear the joys that poison them.

Fielding's ideal is the "great and good" men, who have formed intellectual conceptions of the evil which they cannot feel, and can move out benevolently, forcing sympathetic communication and recognizing its signals. The great and good should be provided with prudence as well as energy, but the former is a dubious quality. Very often the bad for Fielding (as for Aristotle) is the good perverted, and he fears the consequences of power even in the best.[12] He fears that with power the movement outward will too often become exploitive. His great horror, therefore, is aroused by hypocrisy, which he sees as a deliberate distortion of reality, a deliberate blow to our only hope, sympathetic understanding of a world in which we have to do good almost blindly. Reputation is a most important concomitant; it should be our key to the apprehension of the real moral condition of others, but through vanity, hypocrisy, and calumny it becomes another medium of confusion.

As a consequence, Fielding usually points to the *actions* of men, since if these are observed long enough we can approach men's motives, their casts of mind, through all the distortions which the artificialities of society, the lies of others, and their own pretensions have introduced. Virtuous actions usually—though not always—look virtuous; but vice also seeks the appearance of virtue, imposing lies on others as one means of denying them equal humanity. In love lie the greatest capacities for the fulfilment of virtue, since an intense conviction of the humanity of another is combined with an intense concentration of the self outward and an intense satisfaction of the self within. Since love is the greatest good, the perversion of love (as with Wild and his Laetitia) is the worst evil, and it most denies the humanity of another as it most tortures the self.

Briefly, Fielding's central vision of man as enclosed within the self, experiencing happiness or discontent exclusively within the mind, and yet needing to get out of it for the exercise of goodness, has a number of corollaries in his thought. It permeates Fielding's epistemology and psychology, limiting both how people know the world around them and what their reactions to it will be; it tends to combine optimism about the possibilities of happiness within the mind with pessimism about the destinies of the insulated virtuous unless they are miraculously protected from the consequences of their innocence; it combines something of a deterministic approach to human character with a hope that the improvement of environment will allow cultivation of the widespread seeds of goodness.

II

Fielding's System of Psychology

FIELDING, LIKE OTHERS IN HIS DAY—Pope, for example, in the *Essay on Man*—saw the ordinary mind as a battlefield of passions at war with each other and rebellious against the reason. In the good mind, they were ruled by a virtuously-inclined disposition, its role being to act as lord chancellor, as final authority and mediator between them and the reason. The proper attitude toward the operation of one's mind is to recognize the existence of the passions and to try to order them through the reason, which should serve the same function as the Freudian ego, to adjust the violence within to the chaos without. For the virtuous and prudent, such as Allworthy and Amelia, the combination of reason and a good disposition guarantees mental serenity. If the virtuous man is inexperienced, one of the imprudent like Tom or Booth, he must learn to use reason to curb this good will, which can manifest itself too readily in unguarded responses to the wishes of others. In their sexual vagaries, for example, these heroes sin not because of their violent passions but rather out of a good-natured disposition to accede to impassioned ladies. The consequences of yielding, however, often are as bad psychologically as if evil had been intended: both Booth and Tom have exceedingly unhappy moments because of the muddle their good nature or credulity has made of their primary responsibilities. Just as a well-ordered mind undertakes right action, so only right action effects mental serenity.

It is possible, as George Sherburn suggests, to see Fielding as an adherent of the "ruling passion" psychology, which "doubtless developed out of the physiology and psychology of the four humours."[1] Such a view would explain some of the simpler characters in the novels, such as Mrs. Tow-wouse or Thwackum. But what is the ruling passion of Betty the chambermaid in *Joseph Andrews*, to say nothing of such major figures as Blifil or Sophia or Mrs. Bennet? Character is clearly much more complex for Fielding. As often on Fielding's ideas, Henry K. Miller provides the most illuminating discussion of his views of human nature. Fielding, he points out, conceives of people as "having, individually, almost an innate propensity to goodness or to viciousness that . . . subsequent education and circumstances intensify or ameliorate."[2] Mr. Miller discerns three strains in Fielding's views: determinism, the arbitrary disposition of the soul at birth; free will and educability; for some, the permanent effects of early training. Seeing some men as hopelessly corrupt, Fielding concentrates as a practical moralist on those capable of moral education.

Fundamentally, as Miller suggests, Fielding finds men individually "disposed" in one direction or another—toward virtue (theoretically outgoing, though it returns like a boomerang) or toward vice (indrawn selfishness). Indeed, William Empson's comparison of Fielding's ethical system with Calvinism[3] has this justification, that like election to grace, virtue's residence within one mind and not another is ultimately unexplainable. Such arbitrary variations in the moral condition of disposition separate Fielding both from the Hobbes-Mandeville camp and from Shaftesbury's, since both see human nature as basically the same in all people.

Locke had reduced all virtue and vice to pleasure and pain, enlightened by religion; if it were not for the dictates of religion, good would simply be that which causes us pleasure, and evil that which brings pain. Pain, or evil, is a greater motive to action than pleasure, because we may passively allow a pleasure to weaken, or passively not seek to make it greater, while any pain forces immediate attempts at relief. But Locke is more interested in machinery than in ethical precepts; and furthermore, his ruling out of innate ideas involves also a major stress on environment. Environment, presumably subject to the influence of God, molds the moral development of man. If what frees the individual from pain is legally defined as evil—e.g., if he can obtain food only by stealing—then the fault is in the environment.

In the Aristotelian tradition, Locke also finds the passions morally neutral, arguing that the mark of maturity is the ability of the reason to examine the objects which attract or repel the passions. Aversion and desire, which alone evoke the various passions, are themselves rooted in pain and pleasure: "For we love, desire, rejoice, and hope, only in respect of pleasure; we hate, fear, and grieve, only in respect of pain ultimately: in fine, all these passions are moved by things, only as they appear to be the causes of pleasure and pain, or to have pleasure or pain some way or other annexed to them."[4] Though Locke does not say so, it seems that for him—as later for Fielding—the passions are somehow connected to our senses, which are the elementary agents for communicating to the mind the nature of the outer world. The senses make us aware of the objects of pain and pleasure to which the passions are directed.

Accepting the pleasure-pain motivation, Mandeville sees one predisposition, selfishness, universal in mankind, taking its individual shape from the compound of passions to be exercised and satisfied in any one person. He argues that only through thwarting one's own passions and central desires can one be virtuous, insists that no one so acts, and proclaims universal depravity. Mandeville's psychological system is beautifully simple. Man's mind is a chaos of passions feeding his central selfishness: "I believe Man," he writes baldly, "to be a compound of various Passions, that all of them, as they are provoked and come uppermost, govern him by turns, whether he will or no."[5] Of these, pride is in man "so inseparable from his very Essence (how cunningly soever some may learn to hide or disguise it) that without it the Compound he is made of would want one of the chiefest Ingredients . . ." (I, 44-45). With him Fielding shares the over-riding attitude that there is likely to be one central predisposition—though Fielding insists, sometimes in desperation, that it is not universally selfishness.

Shaftesbury agrees that pleasure and pain provide motivation, but argues that there are two natural complexes of desires, one for social and one for personal pleasure. These are groups of "affections," or passions, not really predispositions. Predispositions for Shaftesbury seem to be degrees of affections, not affections themselves; or they may be proportions of affections.[6] Ultimately, the direction or sensitivity of an individual's affections is set by something innate and unexplainable, Shaftesbury's famous moral sense seen in aesthetic terms: "Thus we see, after all, that 'tis not merely what we call *Principle,* but a TASTE, which governs Men. They may think for certain, 'This is *Right,* or that *Wrong:*' They may believe 'This is *a Crime,* or That *a Sin;* This punishable by *Man,* or that by *God:*' yet if the *Savour* of things lies cross to HONESTY; if the *Fancy* be florid, and the *Appetite* high towards the subaltern Beautys and lower Order of worldly Symmetrys and Proportions; the Conduct will infallibly turn this latter way" (III, 177). In the complexity of his psychology, Shaftesbury seems more scientific than Mandeville, though he is equally tendentious. Shaftesbury assumes that the bent, which is formed by the number, variety, and intensity of the passions, may be in any direction, though it "naturally" tends toward the good of both society and the individual. Mandeville is sure only that man is at bottom selfish, the selfishness taking the shape of the dominant passion. Combining the two, Fielding tends to make more use of Shaftesbury's machinery when he is abstractly theorizing, of Mandeville's when he is being practical.

Though Shaftesbury knows that the passions often squabble with each other and with the reason, he tends to see them as good, at the root of human nature, which is itself good. He insists, in response to the Hobbesians and puritans, that man's actions and attitudes are not alone directed by self-interest, but also by caprice, passion, simple good feeling, and so on: " 'Tis hard, that in the Plan or Description of this Clock-work, no Wheel or Ballance should be allow'd on the side of the better and more enlarg'd Affections; that nothing shou'd be understood to be done in *Kindness* or *Generosity;* nothing in *pure Good-Nature* or *Friendship,* or thro any *social* or *natural Affection* of any kind," when actually these natural affections are major motives (I, 115-116).

Individual creatures, he says, naturally have certain "passions and affections" which contribute toward the good of the species: parental love, "Zeal for Posterity, Concern for Propagation and Nurture of the Young, Love of Fellowship and Company, Compassion, mutual Succour, and the rest of this kind" (II, 78). A creature may be driven by natural social affections, or by natural "self-affections," or by those which are neither, and therefore unnatural. Natural affection, the central social virtue, is a passion "which remains as the *Master-Pleasure* and *Conqueror* of the rest" (II, 104). Usually the two sorts of natural affections work together, though at times the self-affection distressingly dominates. A powerful affection inconsistent with the good of the whole species or of society—as, for example, Lady Booby's passion for a footman—"must of necessity create continual Disturbance and Disgust, give an allay to what is immediately enjoy'd in the way of Friendship and Society, and in the end extinguish, in a manner, the very Inclination towards Friendship and human Commerce" (II, 111). On the other hand, "the Consciousness of just Behaviour towards Mankind in general, casts a good reflection on each friendly Affection in particular . . ." (II, 111).

To the neutral system of Locke, the benevolism of Shaftesbury and the latitudinarians,[7] and the reductive misanthropy of Mandeville, Fielding adds the results of his own observations. While these systems are dominant tendencies in his thought, his experience of the inconsistencies of life makes him eclectic, sometimes to the point of contradicting himself. Usually, Fielding thinks that beyond the actual passions which clash with each other and with reason for rule in the mind is one quality, which determines the temper or bent of the individual. But like Shaftesbury, he also at times argues that another principle, a kind of universal sense of right, dispenses internal rewards and punishments. Speaking of his "Essay on the Knowledge of the Characters of Men" in the Preface to the *Miscellanies,* he professes not to understand why men go to so much trouble to be villains when virtue is so easy and pleasurable: "The same righteous judge always annexes a bitter anxiety to the purchases of guilt, whilst it adds a double sweetness to the enjoyments of innocence and virtue: for fear, which all the wise agree is the most wretched of human evils, is, in some degree, always attending on the former, and never can in any manner molest the happiness of the latter" (*Works,* XII, 244). The discomfort of the evil is therefore especially acute; they can see the right, are driven by disposition to the wrong, and, if intelligent, can reflect, in Locke's terminology, on the terrible contrast.

In the essay itself, Fielding says that people are born different from each other:

This original difference will, I think, alone account for that very early and strong inclination to good or evil, which distinguishes different dispositions in children, in their first infancy . . . and . . . in persons, who, from the same education, &c., might be thought to have directed nature the same way; yet, among all these, there subsists . . . so manifest and extreme a difference of inclination or character, that almost obliges us, I think, to acknowledge some unacquired, original distinction, in the nature or soul of one man, from that of another. (*Works,* XIV, 281-2)

After indicating how various inclinations may be shaped by environment (particularly how a bent for deceit is supported by ordinary education), he pauses to examine the sort of phenomenon which Hobbes and Mandeville had used as evidence of man's basic depravity. Seeing a well-dressed person fall in dirt, he says, most people would laugh:

Now, what is this laughter, other than a convulsive ecstasy, occasioned by the contemplation of our own happiness, compared with the unfortunate person's? a pleasure which seems to savour of ill-nature; but as this is one of those first, and as it were spontaneous motions of the soul, which few . . . attend to, and none can prevent; so it doth not properly constitute the character. When we come to reflect on the uneasiness this person suffers, laughter, in a good and delicate mind, will begin to change itself into compassion; and in proportion as this latter operates on us, we may be said to have more or less good-nature. (*Works,* XIV, 287)

I have no need to discuss Fielding's conception of good nature, since it has been so ably treated by others;[8] but it is worth noting that Fielding here provides some sort of disposition, "a good and delicate mind," whose operation to soften innate barbarity constitutes good nature. The selfishness itself is accepted, presumably as our animal heritage, while the goodness and delicacy are the reflective, outgoing, compassionate, and specially human attributes. Every man's mind is thus something of a contest between Yahoos and Houyhnhnms; but if the better principle is well developed or originally dominant, it easily and instinctively controls the worse.

After the predisposing bent, the judge, and/or the innate temper (the resultant of the forces of spontaneous passion and reflective, trained reason), come the passions themselves. They are of various sorts; in some moods Fielding says that it is their proportions that determine virtue, in others their kind, in others the objects to which they become attached. All the passions derive from the desires of the self; when their *object* is the aggrandizement of the self, then they are subsidiaries of pride or vanity. To these last is related Fielding's theme of deception, particularly of self-deception. The twin sources of the ridiculous, as he develops them in the famous preface to *Joseph Andrews,* are vanity (self-deception) and hypocrisy (the attempt to deceive others about oneself).

On self-deception he had many predecessors in classical and near-contemporary analysts of human nature, of whom Locke is the most general and relevant. Locke's epistemology, as I have indicated, works to question the accuracy of our observations; the reason, if it is in control, moves the will and passions to attempt relief from pain, but it may misapprehend or distort the source of the pain, and therefore misdirect the attempt. If the reflective quality is weak, discomfort causes the will to choose temporary alleviation at the price of lasting discontent: though the drunkard knows that he is better off abstaining, he still seeks the satisfaction of drink.[9] If immediate pain is not the spur, a moral man still needs to be judicious about his own motives: his freedom consists in his ability to "suspend" "the satisfaction of any particular desire . . . from determining the will" while he considers whether such determination is consistent with his "real happiness," which is his one permanent goal (II, xxi, 71). The man who cannot reflect and restrain himself in this manner will deceive himself about his own wishes.[10]

As the gallery of deluded characters in Fielding's plays and novels shows, he was well aware of man's tendency to deceive himself both about the rest of the world and about himself; he was also aware of the pain of knowing what is reasonable but being unable to act on this knowledge. These were commonplaces of literary tradition, but they were also peculiarly consistent with Fielding's general views of human nature. In his first play, for example, Malvil says about his beloved, whom another character has been supposing to be a heartless flirt, " 'Sdeath! could I reason thus with myself, I might think so, but I love her above my reason. I see my folly and despise it, and yet cannot shun it" (*Works,* VIII, 18). Wisemore adds to the same effect, "How vain is human reason, when philosophy cannot overcome our passion! when we can see our errors, and yet pursue them" (*Works,* VIII, 61).[11] On one simple level, *Don Quixote in England* (1733) provides the perception of universal delusion which was to be at the core of Fielding's sympathetic comedy. Dr. Drench calls the hero mad, and is answered, "I have heard thee, ignorant wretch, throw that word in my face, with patience. For alas! could it be proved, what were it more than almost all mankind in some degree deserve? Who would doubt the noisy boisterous squire, who was here just now, to be mad? Must not this noble knight here have been mad, to think of marrying his daughter to such a wretch? You, doctor, are mad too, though not so much as your patients. The lawyer here is mad, or he would not have gone into a scuffle, when it is the business of men of his profession to set other men by the ears, and keep clear themselves" (*Works*, XI, 69-70). While none of these characters is necessarily Fielding's spokesman, he is through them evidently presenting a vision of a world wrenched by delusion.

Passions are the source of the delusive imagination, which can in turn provide fancied objects to attract or repel the passions, distorting the outside world or dislocating the normal paths of the passions. As early as *Love in Several Masques*, Fielding already discussed the effect of the psychological context of passion, of which he was to make so much that was delightful in, for example, Betty's yielding to Tow-wouse. Vermilia comments on the relative restraint of a large city:

"I know not why it is, but certainly a woman is the least liable to play the fool here; perhaps the hurry of diversions and company keep the mind in too perpetual a motion to let it fix on one object. Whereas, in the country our ideas are more fixed and more romantic. Courts and cities have few heroes or heroines in love." [Lady Matchless' answer is even more perceptive:] "Ah, Vermilia, let the jealous husband learn from me; there is more danger in woods and purling streams than in an assembly or a playhouse. When a beauteous grove is your theatre, a murmuring cascade your music, nature's flowery landscape your scene, heaven only the spectator, and a pretty fellow the actor—the Lord knows what the play will be." (*Works*, VIII, 31)

In *The Universal Gallant*, an exchange on the subject is more somberly Mandevillian. Mondish tells Mrs. Raffler that "no woman's virtue is proof against the attacks of a resolute lover," to which she answers, "But her fear, her self-love, her coldness, and her vanity" may protect her (*Works*, XI, 142). Reason, in such a case, has triumphed only through a self-destructive alliance with the more vicious passions. As Black George's extended quandary was to show, passions do not simply respond to objects. Rather, the action is likely to be the resultant of all the passional and attractive and repellent forces present. Only among the reasonable can this resultant be examined before it motivates action.

Though reason is susceptible to corruption, it is normally the faculty to which we must entrust control, or else we are lost in madness. In an essay in *The Champion* (February 2, 1740) Fielding describes the difficulty of ruling the passions by the reason and discusses techniques for winning the battle against them. First, following Locke and Shaftesbury, one must look into the mind, to see that there is a balance of the passions, with none out of control. The examination is hard, because the passions are deceitful and may cause us to "mistake avarice for parsimony, profuseness for liberality, pride for honour, and so of the rest"; and if a man thinks he is clear of viciousness, he may simply be succumbing to pride (*Works*, XV, 179). Since the immediate danger is that the passions will dazzle us with the desirability of their object, the treatment, as in Locke and Shaftesbury, is to wait and reflect. The war within the self is as complex and as much in need of strategy as the outer war for virtuous survival. The function of the self-conscious reason within is parallel to that of prudence in one's dealings without; as in Plato, the self is a macrocosm, to which the outside world is a microcosm. As against Plato, however, Fielding sees fortune outside, and haphazard degrees of virtue inside, as contributing to uncertainty.

Those mistaken enough to think the reason a substitute for the passions may make of it a completely repressive agent, and others may conceive it as purely a tool for dominating others. But it has a function in a healthy, well-disposed personality, an essential function in helping to direct the good disposition and in preserving its possessor amidst the dangers of society. The good and active disposition must form a base; otherwise reason is merely available for the purposes of manipulation.

In the *Covent-Garden Journal* at the end of his career, Fielding again eulogizes his favorite form of the element which must unify reason, religion, and passion: outgoing charity. In an exchange of letters, he exhibits the character of the well-disposed though at times fatuous Axylus and his opposite Iago (the same duality as in *Wild*, a dozen years earlier). Summarizing the approaches to the sentimental system of ethics, Axylus says that the lowest men are those full of Pride, Malice, and Envy—but they are not many. Next we go "from the odious to the insipid Character, from those who delight in doing Mischief, to those who have little or no Delight either in the Good or Harm which happeneth to others. Men of this Stamp are so taken up, in contemplating themselves, that the Virtues or Vices, the Happiness or Misery of the rest of Mankind scarce ever employ their Thoughts" (*CGJ*, I, 306). These stoics have been admired as philosophers in the heathen system, but under the "Christian Dispensation" "they will be called to a severe Account . . . for converting solely to their own Use, what was entrusted only to their Care for the general Good" (*CGJ*, I, 307). Next higher are those who claim to be Christians but really do only slight charities; and best are the truly charitable, those who act selflessly. We must go a step higher yet, he says, to enjoy the pleasure of good actions; following Barrow's sermon, "Let us cultivate therefore, my Friend, that excellent Temper of Mind, that Passion which is the Perfection of human Nature, of which the Delight is in doing Good" (*CGJ*, I, 308).

Axylus' emphasis is on right action, as it is all through Fielding. The stoic is repellent because he wraps himself up in his contempt for passion, refusing to participate in the feelings of others. The manipulator is repellent because he merely simulates feelings so that he may use others for his purposes, denying them their own humanity. The ostentatious doer of good deeds is repellent because he is merely feeding his own vanity; though he may be accomplishing something for others, he is unaware of their human existence. The prude or the man who denies life is repellent, since his motive is often envy of the pleasures which others can enjoy or pride in his supposed superiority to them. Equally repellent is the person without sufficient feelings to act or wish to act. Passive virtue is not enough. One must leave the self and do what is right. Here, where Fielding is most theoretical and most didactic in his view of the relations between reason and the passions, he is closest to Shaftesbury and the divines.

But in the discussions of the actual operations and constitution of the passions, as he has seen and experienced them, Fielding is likely to vacillate among systems as one or another seems appropriate. Sometimes, as in his first discussion, the poem to John Hayes,[12] he gives up the attempt to determine the nature of a creature so various, inconsistent, and complex as man. The same man, he says there, is brave one day and a coward the next. Furthermore, at any given time people may seem various:

How passions blended on each other fix,
How vice with virtues, faults with graces mix;

How passions opposite, as sour to sweet,
Shall in one bosom at one moment meet,
With various luck for victory contend,
And now shall carry, and now lose their end. (*Works,* XII, 275)

Nature, working with elementary, atomic passions, gives mixed sources for an action, as mixed colors form Titian's skies:

> So the great artist diff'ring passions joins,
> And love with hatred, fear with rage, combines.

To add to the confusion, nature gives only half of ourselves; we try to appear what we are not, contributing our share of unpredictability:

While Art, repugnant thus to Nature, fights,
The various man appears in different lights. (*Works,* XII, 276)

This early awareness of motivational complexity and uncertainty forms something of a context for Fielding's later delineation of character. In his comic novels, though he at times flaunts the unpredictable—in Adams' occasional irrationality, in Sophia's slight vanity—Fielding works in the direction of consistent characterization. As a thorough Aristotelian more fundamentally concerned than Richardson with moral teaching as integral to the form of the novel, he becomes necessarily more committed to typicality and unity of character.[18] But in *Amelia,* where he even argues that human character is as patterned as art, he is far more concerned with what Ian Watt has called "formal realism," and in consequence finds himself with oddly inconsistent characters on his hands. The Jameses, Miss Matthews, Mrs. Bennet, Mrs. Ellison —all fit the Hayes poem, or the *Champion* paper (December 15, 1739) which says that "The great variety which is found in the nature of man, hath extremely perplexed those writers who have endeavoured to reduce the knowledge of him to a certain science" (*Works,* XV, 102).

With its requirement of three leaders a week, *The Champion* provided Fielding with an opportunity to explore additional aspects of psychology and reflected his ambivalence on the issues which I have already suggested. In a paper of January 3, 1740, for example, we find him arguing the neutrality of certain qualities: they can be good or bad "according to the manner in which they are exerted; or, to speak more philosophically, according to the other qualities with which they are blended in the mind. Valour and wit in a good-natured man are truly amiable, and justly entitle him to the esteem of mankind; but, when they meet with a different disposition, only render the possessor capable of doing greater mischief, and make him a more dangerous enemy to society than he could otherwise have been" (*Works*, XV, 134). This is of course the viewpoint which dominates *Jonathan Wild*.

In another mood, a *Champion* paper of March 15, 1740, takes a contrasting approach closer to the classical moralists than to the recent Christian-latitudinarian tradition: "many more vices and follies arrive in the world through excess than neglect. Passion hurries ten beyond the mark, for one whom indolence holds short of it. . . . Virtue itself, by growing too exuberant and . . . by running to seed changes its very nature, and becomes a most pernicious weed of a most beautiful flower" (*Works*, XV, 243-4). Here is a dislike for enthusiasm as thorough as Horace's or Shaftesbury's, an attitude that is closely related to Fielding's suspicion in his novels of all those who profess intense religious motivations. Captain Ahab's destruction by a zeal against evil was not unsuspected before Melville. Despite the variations in Fielding's attitude, at no time does he approve of unregulated expression of the passions, since their effects on others and on the self must be vicious.

In the "Essay on the Knowledge of the Characters of Men" Fielding takes as his subject the removal of the distortions which pride and vanity have made current. People even slightly disposed toward deceit are confirmed in this odious quality, he says, by prudential educations which teach them to wear masks. To teach the innocently good how to see through the disguises is the purpose of the essay. At this early stage of his career he thinks such a concentrated course is possible, since "the passions of men do commonly imprint sufficient marks on the countenance; and it is owing chiefly to want of skill in the observer that physiognomy is of so little use and credit in the world" (*Works*, XIV, 284). As often when Fielding is self-consciously practical, he follows the Mandevillian reduction, with the important qualification that he assumes his readers and others to be exempt from domination by pride.

To begin with, he warns against gravity of appearance, which so often covers folly: "The affections which it indicates, and which we shall seldom err in suspecting to lie under it, are pride, ill-nature and cunning" (*Works*, XIV, 285). Another appearance, a "glavering, sneering smile," which people think "a sign of good-nature," "is generally a compound of malice and fraud, and as surely indicates a bad heart, as a galloping pulse doth a fever" (*Works*, XIV, 285). Nature's signs, like "that sprightly and penetrating look, which is almost a certain token of understanding," are subtle and may escape notice; but affectations are so thickly laid on that they often deceive the observer. Most people are a mixture of good and bad; and consequently, the Mandevillian base of their responses needs to be overcome, evidently through the strengthening of their outgoing impulses. One basis for real friendship, for example, is esteem, but esteem must first conquer the great obstacle of pride: "it is an involuntary affection, rather apt to give us pain than pleasure, and therefore meets with no encouragement in our minds, which it creeps into by small and almost imperceptible degrees" (*Works*, XIV, 292). In this essay Fielding passes his earlier helpless conclusion that man is unpredictable and goes on to argue that human character and action are the consequences—through an almost arithmetic addition and cancelation—of specific passions and affections and dispositions. His essay is designed for practical advice, not for a theoretical scheme to cover all the possibilities.

"Of the Remedy of Affliction for the Loss of Our Friends," written out of Fielding's own terrible experience, is his most specific attempt to analyze the passions at work. It again shows the ambiguity of his view, combining sympathy for the warmth which the passions give with insistence that their indulgence leads to blind self-enclosure. Despite the arguments of the stoics, he says, calmness in the face of death of loved ones "is owing to mere insensibility; to a depravity of the heart, not goodness of the understanding" (*Works*, XVI, 99). Sadly, he agrees that time is the ultimate healer: "With whatever violence our passions at first attack us they will in time subside. It is then that reason is to be called to our assistance, and we should use every suggestion which it can lend to our relief; our utmost force being to be exerted to repel and subdue an enemy when he begins to retreat: this, indeed, one would imagine, should want little or no persuasion to recommend it; inasmuch as we all naturally pursue happiness and avoid misery" (*Works*, XVI, 102). Though he has rejected Cicero and the stoics, nonetheless he hopes for the possibility of some element of control. Instead of indulging grief indefinitely, we must try to avoid whatever reminds us of the dead beloved; we must help time to cure us, not fight the cure. The real medicine for this grief, "as well as every other mental disorder, is to be dispensed to us by philosophy and religion" (*Works*, XVI, 104). Where an excess of concern for oneself—pride and vanity—leads directly to social illnesses, an excess of grief for others (which may be related to delusive recollections of one's own felicity) leads to private madness. Since its motive is better, it must be treated more kindly, helped and not punished—but it must also be restrained. Man's duty is to act in the real world, not to be closed off against it.

Fielding's "Essay on Conversation" is relevant here, since "conversation," an aspect of good breeding, is also a formal arrangement for taking men out of themselves into an awareness of the existence—and the human rights—of others. Following Shaftesbury closely, he considers good breeding a social mechanism to provide a maximum of individual happiness. In society, if properly constituted, is man's ideal condition; there the individual's happiness is necessarily increased in proportion as he contributes to the happiness of others. One major element in such a successful society is good breeding, "the art of pleasing, or contributing as much as possible to the ease and happiness of those with whom you converse" (*Works*, XIV, 299).

The central rule of social behavior, and therefore of good breeding, is to do unto others as they would like to be done by; but the problem is to tell how men would be done by. If men do not know their own desires, they may mistake those of others. To ensure the proper deference to the expectations of its members, society has developed formal rules of behavior and formal divisions into ranks. While these rules have no basis in absolute merit, they codify expectations and keep the peace. At table, for example, orders of precedence formalize the views which people have been bred to have of themselves. There, "regard is rather to be had to birth than fortune; for though purse-pride is forward enough to exalt itself, it bears a degradation with more secret comfort and ease than the former, as being more inwardly satisfied with itself, and less apprehensive of neglect or contempt" (*Works*, XIV, 254). The mental peace, not the inalienable right, of the gentry is to be considered. Society is to be cemented by mutual good will, with the rules of good breeding as guides to good will.

Vice, Fielding continues, usually includes ill-nature (the disposition, which seems antecedent to the passions themselves); if the good-natured man is stupid he may be proud, "but arrogant and insolent he cannot be" (Works, XIV, 261). The aim of contempt is to expose the victim to shame, which gives such a shock to his being as to be destructive of his identity. Since "this contempt of others is the truest symptom of a base and a bad heart" (Works, XIV, 263), the concept of good breeding is organically related to the Lockean idea of symptoms, of the outer action from which we are to guess the internal constitution. At the core of the mind is the disposition, which seems to shape the passions at some times, and at others is the total configuration of the passions. It presumably includes something of reason, though a well-disposed man may be stupid; and ultimately it is deducible from the outer appearance and actions of the person. Good breeding, like an open, eager countenance, is to the early Fielding a symptom of a good-natured willingness to fulfill the proper expectations of others.

Jonathan Wild is much more consistent as well as much simpler than the essays in the Miscellanies in its endorsement and illustration of the straightforward "disposition" view of psychology. The protagonist is an amusing monster of self-enclosed vanity with no concern at all for the humanity of others. The Heartfrees, in contrast to Wild and his Laetitia (who are both careful to simulate the proper passions), readily respond with outgoing joy to all symptoms of goodness. In general, the virtuous show emotion much more spontaneously than the evil, largely because their emotions, which are not evidently selfish, give peace rather than turmoil and receive the acknowledgment of society. Being creditable, these emotions result in self-satisfaction, not disturbance.

The guilty mind is completely within a ferocious world which it has itself constructed; the injured person should look outside for prudential reasons, and for the materials of moral action, but for peace he need go no further than his own mind. In prison Heartfree "enjoyed a quiet, undisturbed repose," while Wild could not sleep. Wild, on the other hand, in a constant state of war with the rest of humanity, was not at peace even on the rare occasions when he wanted to be. Though he and Tishy conclude a marital fight by deciding to be amiably indifferent for the future, they hate each other too much to refrain from mutual plaguing. In his professional life Wild "was under a continual alarm of frights, and fears, and jealousies," alert to be the first to betray: "so much doth it behove all great men to be eternally on their guard, and expeditious in the execution of their purposes; while none but the weak and honest can indulge themselves in remissness or repose" (III, xiv). Selfishness, as personified in Wild, is a source of meaningless and unending turmoil, leading only to short-lived moments of passional satiety, as against the steady content of the outwardly disposed.

In the reform tracts of Fielding's last half dozen years, he tended toward a psychological approach to morality and social problems. Discussing the treatment of serious offenders in his *Proposal for . . . Provision for the Poor,* he counsels fasting and solitude as better preliminary cures for criminality than shame, "for by once inflicting shame on a criminal we forever remove that fear of it, which is one very strong preservative against doing evil" (*Works,* XIII, 183). If we consider also the punitive measures of the gypsy king in *Tom Jones,* it seems that the Mandevillian assumption of competitive vanity as the spur to all bad actions (and to some good ones as well) consistently underlay Fielding's practical advice on reward and punishment. His poor, who might otherwise be unemployed and dangerous, are to live in monastic workhouse-prisons on the perimeter of London. They are to be liberally dosed with religious instruction, to which they will be ideally receptive: "Hope and fear, two very strong and active passions, will hardly find a fuller or more adequate object to amuse and employ them; this more especially in a place where there will be so little of temptation to rouse or to gratify the evil inclinations of human nature; where men will find so few of those good things of this world, for which the other is every day bartered; and where they will have no encouragement, from the example of their betters, to make so prudent an exchange" (*Works,* XIII, 186-7). Their psychological condition will be perfectly suitable for moral improvement, though it may strike us as odd that their social usefulness is predicated on their isolation from society. It is a measure of Fielding's despair that he is willing at the end of his life to sacrifice the integrated society for peace.

The *Increase of Robbers* (1751) develops at length the synthesis of social psychology, economics, and political theory which Fielding sees as determining the nature of society. Behind it is the Platonic assumption of the body politic as a version of the individual mind which is ideally self-contained through a balance of forces, a temperate and contented whole, able to aspire after the good. When luxury seeps down from the upper classes to the tradesman or laborer, Fielding says, it leads to robbery, "to which not only the motive of want but of shame conduces; for there is no greater degree of shame than the tradesman generally feels at the first inability to make his regular payments; nor is there any difficulty which he would not undergo to avoid it" (*Works,* XIII, 22). Whatever may explain individual human nature, a society seems most comprehensible in Mandevillian terms: "Now the two great motives to luxury, in the mind of man, are vanity and voluptuousness" (*Works,* XIII, 23). The former is minor with the lower orders, for though they have as much vanity as their betters, the chances of gratifying this passion are so slight that it is sublimated. Consequently, they are led to luxury through love of pleasure—the nation's ruling passion, according to Fielding's *Charge to the Grand Jury* (1749)—and so he wants restrictions on public amusements and holidays.

Having been moved to crime by shame and the love of pleasure, two passions which they insist on immediately gratifying, robbers are encouraged by the tenderheartedness of the virtuous, which prevents them from exacting the death penalty. Fielding stops for a eulogy of "a tender-hearted and compassionate disposition," which is at the same time both natural and Christian: "Indeed the passion of love or benevolence, whence this admirable disposition arises, seems to be the only human passion that is in itself simply and absolutely good; and in Plato's commonwealth, or (which is more) in a society acting up to the rules of Christianity, no danger could arise from the highest excess of this virtue" (*Works,* XIII, 110). But in actual human societies, rascals swarm to take advantage of this benevolence, so that it behoves the good-natured man "to restrain the impetuosity of his benevolence, carefully to select the objects of his passion, and not by too unbounded and indiscriminate an indulgence to give the reins to a courser which will infallibly carry him into the ambuscades of the enemy" (*Works,* XIII, 110). The problem in society is the same as in individuals—benevolence without prudence, as Fielding had been arguing since the *Miscellanies,* is an invitation to imposition. Both individuals and groups must learn to examine the objects of passion, or man and his society will be lost in chaos.

His discussion of the nature and processes of executions is again in terms of the psychology of prisoner, jury, and public. A public execution, he says, becomes a scene of triumph and admiration for the criminal, who is its hero. Shame was intended by public executions, but the effect is the opposite, since the idea of death is so terrifying that it absorbs all other ideas in the mind (as various contemporary aestheticians pointed out in developing the theory of the sublime in literature). The best way to achieve the psychological deterrent, to raise terror without any pity or admiration, would be through swift execution, which would show the criminal not as a suffering or triumphing man, a tragic hero, but as non-human, a thing. If the crime "be of an atrocious kind, the resentment of mankind being warm, would pursue the criminal to his last end, and all pity for the offender would be lost in detestation of the offence"; but after a long delay, "the punishment and not the crime is considered; and no good mind can avoid compassionating a set of wretches who are put to death we know not why, unless, as it almost appears, to make a holiday for, and to entertain, the mob" (*Works,* XIII, 123). In advising the use of hope and fear for the possibly godless poor, and of terror for the potentially criminal, Fielding is suggesting psychological manipulation of the lower orders, not of the thoughtful and well bred. He does not repudiate Locke and Shaftesbury, who recommended reflective introspection when the passions are intensely affected; but he is assuming that the lower orders, largely incapable of reflection, need to be controlled through direct appeals to the appropriate passions.[14]

The passions, then, are dangerous, though Fielding at times points out that good ones exist, or that something to be thought of as a good disposition makes the active energies, whatever they may be called, show themselves outside the mind in a process which helps calm the mind. The shaping of energies toward good is at times achieved by this good disposition, at times by reason, and always by religion when that is present. It is not clear, however, whether these are three different things or whether the disposition includes a tendency toward the operation of reason and religion; for that matter, though "reason" is usually a mechanism for dealing with social reality, and to that extent includes "prudence," many of his characters, notably the younger good men, are described as having excellent minds, and yet in need of learning prudence. Reason would then seem, like disposition, innate, whereas prudence is that constituent of it which can be learned from experience or precept. But prudence where it is an original part of the disposition is likely to become more and more the sign of selfishness, as with Wild and Tishy.

In Fielding's psychological system, a man's moral condition is ultimately determined by his disposition, which is predominantly either selfish or charitable.[15] This is given: a congenital orientation of the mind. People, therefore, differ fundamentally from each other. On the basis of his experience, Fielding again and again declares that human nature arbitrarily varies, and he thereby importantly differs from both the Mandevillian and the Shaftesburian views, which we normally see as highly influential in the century.[16]

The ultimate disposition (which is so abstract that it can only be described as selfish-indrawn or charitable-outgoing) may manifest itself clinically in a ruling passion such as avarice or ambition, if the disposition is selfish. If outgoing, the disposition remains general, suitable, say, for sexual love in youth, the disbursal of charity, an open responsiveness to the wishes of others. In a sense, the good disposition is the One, which is always the same under a variety of forms; the bad, the many passions which can dominate the mind. As deep within the self as the disposition, Fielding sometimes suggests, is a uniform, universal sense of right, a conscience, which dispenses mental pain or pleasure in response to the evil or good which man does. The disposition, in this view, is thus the differentiating factor in mankind, while the conscience is uniform, differing in degree but not in kind among individuals. However, the conscience may simply be a name to describe a sense of harmony or disharmony in the mind, not a separate faculty.

As a bow to the Hobbesians, Fielding does a few times grant the likelihood that we may all contain a malicious element—a "spontaneous motion of the soul"—which delights at least briefly in the discomfiture of another. But such an element acts involuntarily in the well-disposed man, and is replaced by a benevolent response as soon as he has time to be thoughtful. Fielding needs this instinctive element so that his system can cover all observable reality; but when he presented that reality in his novels, he never showed such spontaneous malice motivating his virtuous characters (as against, say, Smollett, who uses it as his most immediately discernible comic principle).

The most attractive figures in Fielding's miscellaneous writings —Boncour, the young heroes of the plays, Heartfree and his wife, Axylus of the *Covent-Garden Journal*, and so on—are governed by a disposition toward good nature and the sense of right, and are able to dominate and form their passions toward active benevolence. But most people have an element of ruling passion to distort their minds from the true center. If carried back to the core of the self, these ruling passions—always bad in that they cause us to mistake reality—will be subsumed under vanity. Most men in significant degrees, and all men at least slightly, wish to appear flawless to appease their internal sense of rightness and their sense of self. The central passion of vanity—and all its subsidiary passions like ambition, lust, and avarice—may therefore endanger anyone by interfering with his primary need, which is to see reality clearly so that he can act in it effectively.

All the passions, even the useful ones like hope and fear, can be delusive agents. They can prompt the imagination—always a dangerous faculty—to substitute a world different from actuality for their subject to act in, rendering men incompetents who can range morally from Don Quixote and Parson Adams on one end to Wild and Blifil on the other. The moral difference lies at least partly in the extent to which a man consciously distorts the world for others; but all distort it at least slightly for themselves.

Within sane and relatively well-disposed people, the reason, as the mechanism for relating man to reality, frequently engages in battle with the passions. Its best weapon, which Fielding borrowed from Locke and Shaftesbury, is careful introspection, combined with delay in pursuing the object desired by the passions. The reason is therefore largely a conscious, even a self-conscious, quality which functions to make the nature and workings of the passions also conscious. It is thus an instrument for revealing internal as well as external reality. If the reason is healthy, it can cause pain when it discovers that a passion other than love is dominant or that an improper act has been done, or pleasure when the mind is operating harmoniously in consonance with the outer world. If it has been weakened by dominant passions, the mind is diseased and in pain. Where such passion-dominated minds act in society, they disrupt (as with calumny), and society must legislate to protect itself.

Theoretically, Fielding sometimes considers the passions neutral, in accordance with the views of Aristotle, Locke, and the latitudinarians. Actually, however, he seems to disapprove of all of those which can in any way nourish vanity or pride, which is to say all but love or good nature, if that may be called a passion which more frequently seems to be a disposition. While the scheme would abstractly assume a reservoir of passions, channeled by a superior good or bad disposition, he often writes as if the good disposition is parallel to and separate from the passions, which are available only to the bad. In some benevolent characters in the plays, such as Boncour, a certain aggressive strength is notable, but not at the expense of others; and they suffer from none of the other passions associated with vanity. Where passions are strong, they manifest themselves in the appearance of the mask which their subject puts on; where reason and good nature rule, there is no cover on the frank features.

But even good people can and do have passions, Fielding always concludes. Such people are, however, notable for the balance and control which they exhibit, for their avoidance of either internal or external distortion. Complete calmness in response to powerful appeals to passion—such as extreme distress or death of a fellow human being—"is mere insensibility." If we cannot provide help, if we cannot remedy the inevitable, then our mental stability must be disturbed in the direction of pain, and only time combined with the eventual operation of reason can console us. But for the well-disposed person only such awareness of the misery of others which we cannot cure, or of loss of good, or of our own heedless bad actions (which must be accidental) can cause mental pain. Constant brooding over the cause of this pain delays the application of reason and therefore delays the return to mental peace—as witness the permanently distorted Man of the Hill.

Since vanity is the central selfish passion, terror and shame or the fear of shame may be society's best weapons for controlling selfish aggression by individuals. Similarly, disdain is the most thorough repudiation of the self of another, and should be restrained by society except as punishment for actions so odious as to be inhuman. Executions should be so managed as to arouse in the audience the mental responses called on by the sublime in literature as it is manifest in the greatest tragedies. Their minds should be completely filled with a sympathetic terror, to prevent their ever earning such a fate for themselves. Religion, which may exist within the mind on a level parallel to disposition, reason, and conscience, is particularly useful to society, since it meets vanity with the lure of hope and the threat of fear. In this way, religion can be a powerful unifying factor within as well as a limiting factor without. At least as importantly, combined with reason it can support, direct, and reward good nature as it sallies out to perform right actions.

In society, the class system and training in decorous behavior have been developed to prevent the aggressive pride of individuals from destroying human intercourse. While Fielding never pretends that the division into classes is based on any fundamental distinctions in nature, he nonetheless insists on its necessity. Like Plato, he sees the operation of a good society as the equivalent of a harmonious mind; but he does not parallel the reason with the aristocrats or the passions with the lower orders, though he believes that their training and education may lead in these directions. Furthermore, society is like the individual in that it has enough good seeds to achieve order and fruitfulness if it should be provided with an intense desire for reform. The aim of society is, then, to reach its optimum moral condition, so that it can be a fit context for the moral flowering of its members.

III

Self-enclosure in the Novels

IN THE FAMOUS preface to *Joseph Andrews* the derivation of the ridiculous from affectation, which in turn is derived from vanity or hypocrisy, immediately relates Fielding's subject and technique to his sense of psychological enclosure. Vanity is a distorted view of the self and of outer reality arising from an inability to see oneself in proper perspective; hypocrisy, an attempt to mislead others —who are also assumed to be masqueraders—as they try to compare themselves with us. In either case, preoccupation with the self causes, and manifests itself in, limited ways of knowing: we can know mainly elements outside ourselves which correspond to elements within.

All through *Joseph Andrews* major plot issues depend on the enclosure of the self and the consequent comic lack of communication. The first significant episode, Lady Booby's attempted seduction of Joseph, involves three failures to see outside the self: her failure to recognize that she is subject to an animal desire which levels her with others of her species; her inability to communicate her feelings clearly to Joseph, at least in the first scene; and hilarious problems of communication with her serving woman Slipslop, who recognizes the animal lust and snobbery— since she shares both in cruder form—but cannot tell which element is dominant in Lady Booby. In turn, Lady Booby is unable to imagine for Joseph any orientation notably different from her own, any response to sex but the exploitive one which would make her a highly desirable conquest for a footman. At the end of the novel, when the peddler tells the story that makes Joseph and Fanny brother and sister, everyone believes him, except Pamela, who had never heard her parents mention another child, "and except the Lady Booby, who suspected the falsehood of the story from her ardent desire that it should be true; and Joseph, who feared its truth from his earnest wishes that it might prove false" (IV, xiii).

Between beginning and end, incident after incident shows that our knowledge of the outside world reflects what is within ourselves. In one sequence, for example, Parson Trulliber, at the moment eager to sell hogs, unhesitatingly accepts his wife's identification of Adams as a hog buyer. Besides the Lockean associationist psychology, we are also presented with the pervasive moral issue of seeing others simply as ministrants to our needs and desires. Trulliber is taken up with his own "greatness and importance," which is fed both by his wealth and by his wife's willingness to yield her identity to serve and admire him. But the yielding is not so slavish and self-effacing as it at first seems. He is evidently sexually prodigious, so that he serves her lust while she satisfies his pride. In Fielding's novels, such a modus vivendi is often routine humanity's parody of the unusual felicity of the heroes. We rub along, he shows, substituting the exhibition of parallel passions for the intersection of good dispositions which constitutes true communication.

Early in *Tom Jones*, in general a work much more integrated than its predecessor, we see in more detail how different characteristics condition different ways of knowing and understanding the world of events. Furthermore, the plot itself is evidently based on this view of character. At the very beginning, Mrs. Wilkins concludes at once that some local slut is laying her bastard to Allworthy; Allworthy, responsive to a wider range of feelings, thinks the unknown mother has taken the wisest way of providing for her child. Notable evidence of the consciousness of Fielding's intention is his development of Bridget as exactly the sort of woman who might have been most violent at the expense of the bastard, but who is instead quite tolerant. Her attitude is triumphantly explained at the end, but its unexpectedness in the beginning neatly alerts us to the problem of psychological orientation. Square and Thwackum, unable to see out of self-bounded minds, attempt to ingratiate themselves with her by beating and maligning Tom: "nay, the more civility she showed him, the more they conceived she detested him, and the surer schemes she was laying for his ruin: for as they thought it her interest to hate him, it was very difficult for her to persuade them she did not" (III, vi). Fielding can play any number of characters in the game of relative self-enclosure, as we see in the responses of Square, Thwackum, Allworthy, Western, Tom, Sophia, and Blifil to the incident of Sophia's bird.

When the main characters are old enough to justify a discussion of love, Fielding points out that self-enclosure may make us doubt its existence. But if we do not recognize ourselves as having a certain passion, we should not conclude that no one has it. Furthermore, the refusal to acknowledge the existence of feelings we do not share is an example of our vanity, of our adulation of our own minds (VI, i). These postulates, fundamental to Fielding's moral and psychological themes and therefore to his entire plot, are specifically comments on the remainder of Book VI, which has much to say about the Western family's concern over the love life of Sophia.

The issue of self-enclosure is here not only integrated with the plot, but even central to it. It is Mrs. Western's misconception, forced on a basically kind woman by decades of living in a milieu where the distortion of communication is a formal art, which causes the love involvement in the novel, more immediately which precipitates Sophia's family troubles and Tom's exile. Mrs. Western, whose leitmotif is the boast of perceptiveness, is superbly blind, completely unable to understand a genuine emotion, because she works by rules of town affectations. Applying these carefully, she is certain that Sophia loves Blifil. Sophia, young as she is, intuitively knows the difficulty of agreeing on external reality: she asks, "is it possible my father and you, madam, can see with my eyes?" and the secret is out (VI, v).

Western and his sister immediately demonstrate that Sophia's surprise is justified. Blinded by his assumption that equality of fortune is as necessary in marriage as difference in sex, Western "had no more apprehension of his daughter's falling in love with a poor man than with any animal of a different species" (VI, ix). Mrs. Western also could reflect only her background; she had been lecturing Sophia on prudence, "recommending to her the example of the polite world," in which love was ridiculed, and marriage seen as a business by women. Since she can see the match with Blifil only in economic and political terms (the union of two great families), she cannot imagine Sophia's concern for happiness and virtue; Sophia, in turn, is unable to understand her aunt (VII, iii). In the long run, the good and sane person, as Fielding presents him, may learn through superior experience and developing prudence how to estimate the attitudes, evil in one way or another, which are foreign to him. The distorted person, either innately subject to passion or completely formed by his environment, can never really understand the serene one, and that is why it is so hard for evil or folly to thrive indefinitely.

Selfish enclosure, as Fielding sees our lives, is normal for many, so casually and unconsciously assumed, so fundamental to their ways of apprehending anything, that they are startled at the notion of its being waived. Honour, for example, is horrified when Sophia talks of suicide: "To be sure it can be nothing but the devil which can put such wicked thoughts into the head of anybody; for certainly it is less wicked to hurt all the world than one's own dear self" (VII, vii). The landlady of an inn ingenuously builds up a twentieth-century system of political economy on the same principle. She wants the army to kill all the enemy, for "To be sure it is natural for us to wish our enemies dead that the wars may be at an end, and our taxes be lowered" (VII, xiii). Such unconscious revelation of preoccupation with self forms one of Fielding's staple comic devices; the landlady's statement, unexpected and yet appropriate, depends as much on ignorance of the humanity of others as do the attitudes of Lady Booby and Slipslop.

So pervasive is self in the world of *Tom Jones* that it cuts us off from objective understanding of events as they happen to us, even when we have no intention of distorting these events. Tom tells Partridge all that relates to his dismissal, except that he omits the damning events of his day of drunkenness. He did not intend to hide the truth, says Fielding, who we must remember was an experienced lawyer and a part-time Mandevillian, but "let a man be never so honest, the account of his own conduct will, in spite of himself, be so very favourable" that his vices will vanish in the telling (VIII, v). "For though the facts themselves may appear, yet so different will be the motives, circumstances, and consequences, when a man tell his own story, and when his enemy tells it, that we scarce can recognize the facts to be one and the same" (VIII, v).

Limited by his own understanding of the events, which shows him innocent of any wrongdoing or even any evidences of wrongdoing, Tom unintentionally deceives Partridge. Thinking over the story, Partridge cannot imagine a good reason for Allworthy to turn out his own son (which Partridge, evaluating Allworthy's actions on the basis of his own nature, must believe Tom to be): "He concluded, therefore, that the whole was a fiction, and that Jones, of whom he had often from his correspondents heard the wildest character, had in reality run away from his father." Consequently, he thought that if he could bring Tom back home he himself would be reinstated in favor (VIII, vii). Furthermore, Partridge was so committed to the Jacobite cause that he misunderstood Tom's political attitude toward the rebellion. Even if Tom's phrasing had been unambiguous, Fielding says, Partridge would have come to the same conclusion, "being persuaded as he was that the whole nation were of the same inclination in their hearts" (VIII, ix). And so another major plot development in the novel, the joining of the two memorable companions, is a consequence of weakness of communication owing to concern with the self. As with the love complications (initiated by Mrs. Western's misunderstandings), Fielding takes as his underlying plot simple romantic elements—the search for a father, the crossed love between a poor man and a rich girl[1]—but develops it in terms of his realistic concerns, primarily those involved in getting out of the enclosed self.

Blamably unsuspicious, Tom believes Partridge's self-justifications and his claim that he was not Tom's father. There are only two ways to achieve suspicion, says Fielding, in one of a number of passages to the same effect in his writings: from experience and by nature. The latter, he says in an ironic reference to the sympathetic imagination, is better, "for a man who hath been imposed on by ever so many, may still hope to find others more honest; whereas he who receives certain necessary admonitions from within, that this is impossible, must have very little understanding indeed, if he ever renders himself liable to be once deceived" (VIII, vii). Tom, unsuspicious by nature, was too young and heedless to have learned suspicion through prudence. Fielding deliberately protects him from such learning, leaving it to the old Man of the Hill, his surrogate, who has made of suspicion a way of life occasioned by his unrelieved disillusionment and his consequent hatred of mankind. His deliberate isolation from hu-

manity, placed at the center of the novel, becomes a major symbol
of self-enclosure.

The high point of the comic plot, the complicated maneuver-
ing at the inn at Upton, exploits the contrast between self-enclosure and virtuous radiation from within. The episode begins with
the landlady's violent refusal to allow Mrs. Waters to enter the
inn, on the ground that she serves no poor and ragged whores. As
we learn, the moral objection is quite justified; but since the
economic one is not, the landlady, whose mind is bounded by
greed, is complacent. Mrs. Waters, in the mock-epic battle of love,
understands Tom in the same way that he more properly understands the steak. Good-naturedly responding to her desires—since
he is capable of love, and the sexual appetite, as part of love, is
one of his passions—he forgets his more intense dedication to
Sophia. Fitzpatrick, dominated by jealous resentment, cannot understand that the world contains more than one unaccompanied
woman and barges into the wrong room. Squire Western, alone in
his own microcosm, erupts wherever he can imagine a woman to
be, sure he will find his daughter. Mrs. Fitzpatrick, willing to betray her cousin's lover to her uncle for protection, wastes her
breath, since he is insulated against all runaway women. Partridge
and Mrs. Honour, both interested in prestige above all, give away
the secrets that their superiors are determined to keep. Sophia,
more concerned for Tom's respect than disturbed by his sexual
misbehavior, blames him for bandying her name everywhere,
one offense of which he is innocent. In general, the burlesque effects of these big scenes derive primarily from passions and preoccupations on the part of individuals and from the efforts of
some of them to distort reality for everyone else. In the terms of
the preface to *Joseph Andrews,* even Tom and Sophia suffer
slightly from vanity; but they, the chambermaid, Fitzpatrick, and
the mindless Squire Western are at least free of the pervasive
hypocrisy.

On more subtle levels, the distortions in favor of the self, both
voluntary and involuntary, continue to affect communication. To
pick one conspicuous example among many, in the whole course
of Mrs. Fitzpatrick's autobiographical narrative to Sophia, she
does not mention the lord who has befriended her and in whose
coach they are to travel—for obvious reasons. Sophia, for her part,
tells Mrs. Fitzpatrick her own story, which Fielding does not

repeat: "One remark, however, I cannot forbear making on her narrative, namely, that she made no more mention of Jones, from the beginning to the end, than if there had been no such person alive. This I will neither endeavor to account for nor to excuse" (XI, viii).

The sympathetic recognition of our own characteristics in others and the limitations developed by environment remain central psychological and moral ideas throughout the novel. Again to use one example of many, Fielding tells us that Dowling was not really a bad fellow, for a lawyer: "an attorney may feel all the miseries and distresses of his fellow-creatures, provided he happens not to be concerned against them" (XII, x). That social artifact, an occupation, such as law or inn-keeping or domestic service, may color our views of others and ourselves, much affecting our basic mental and moral constitution. Dowling estimates Tom's attitude toward Blifil on the basis of the legal assumption of universal selfishness: Tom had every right to expect a considerable legacy from Allworthy, "if not the whole; nay, if you had expected the whole, I should not have blamed you; for certainly all men are for getting as much as they can, and they are not to be blamed on that account" (XII, x). Tom convincingly repudiates such selfish motives, to the lawyer's delight: though he tries to hide his friendly response, "it is certain he secretly approved as much of his sentiments as he understood, and really felt a very strong impulse of compassion for him" (XII, x). Nonetheless, he willingly enters a conspiracy to destroy Tom, allowing his selfishness and his principles of legal neutrality to outweigh the secret impulses of humanity. But Fielding wants us to know that even corrupt people may have "spontaneous motions of the soul" toward good, just as his paragons may be caught in contrary impulses. The tests are action and the motive for action; all else is irrelevant.

In the denouement as in all the other significant plot developments, the novel asserts the need and yet warns of the consequences of straying out of the self to act in a dangerous world. All of Tom's faults have derived from overdoing the emission of virtue, from incautiously obliging everyone. Providentially, he is saved from the fruits of this carelessness and shown the horror to which it might expose him. His good-natured involvement with Mrs. Waters apparently leads to his breaking the most extreme taboo, against incest, which is cursed by both religion and society;

his possible killing of Fitzpatrick allows him the equally horrible vision of his being a criminal—with religion and conscience and even law against him despite society's approval of the dueling code. When the various truths are revealed—largely by people, like Jenny Jones and Dowling, through whose environment enough decency has seeped to permit a response to Tom's good will—his exercise of outgoing goodness persuades Sophia and, through Mrs. Miller, Allworthy, while Blifil's self-enclosure guarantees his downfall with his exposure. Tom is left at the end the respected and wealthy possessor of a beautiful wife and a serene and loving mind, "the happiest of all mankind."

The hero and heroine in *Amelia*, like those in the other novels, survive all dangers because their disposition is toward good; and all through their felicity or lack of it seems dependent exclusively on their consciousness of having acted well or ill. Amelia herself, being dutifully and unquestioningly religious, never has much to disturb her happiness. Booth, however, looks at his career with legal eyes, thereby committing the error which lawyer Fielding had shown us in the previous novels. Since he thought himself overly mistreated by fortune, Booth had religious doubts: "A dangerous way of reasoning, in which our conclusions are not only too hasty, from an imperfect view of things, but we are likewise liable to much error from partiality to ourselves, viewing our virtues and vices as through a perspective, in which we turn the glass always to our own advantage, so as to diminish the one, and as greatly to magnify the other" (I, iii).

Ways of perceiving and of reacting emotionally are here as in the other novels dependent on the prejudices and emotional constitution of the perceiver. Booth's opening involvement with Miss Matthews, which develops as a distant echo of Aeneas' with Dido,[2] is effected largely by wilful delusion on the part of both. Miss Matthews fancies herself into romantic ecstasies at Booth's account of his love, and Booth much exaggerates the gentility of his protectress in the enchanted jail. In describing Booth's emotions when he is rescued from jail and Miss Matthews, Fielding reaffirms the enclosed, psychological nature of happiness or distress. It is hard to tell the degree of another's happiness "from the knowledge of external circumstances"; sometimes a little speck of black in the bright colors deadens the whole, and "when all without looks dark and dismal, there is often a secret ray of light within the mind, which turns every thing to real joy and gladness" (IV, iii). Booth, having acted badly, is dominated by the speck of black even though he is now free; Amelia, despite the squalor which she faces, is rewarded for her virtue by the secret ray. The substitution of rays and specks for lord chancellors seems—aside from its suitability for a work in various flowing shades of gray rather than in the brilliant clarity and color of *Tom Jones*—a step even further from a formal system of psychology, and therefore a step closer to observation of confused actuality.

As in the other novels, deception and general misapprehension in the communication of motives, plans, and events are central to the action. Miss Matthews initiates some of Booth's most aggravating difficulties by telling Colonel James distorted versions of what Booth has said about him. Amelia, unaware of the intrigue, thinks that she has persuaded Booth to ask James about his aloofness, whereas Booth's discovery of its roots in rivalry over Miss Matthews has apparently removed it. Booth, Mrs. Bennet, James, Bath, the noble lord, even the models of virtue Amelia, Atkinson, and Harrison at various times engage in deceptions, the bad for their own ends, the good to protect others, and almost all at times to fool themselves in the interests of great or little shares of vanity.

Delusion develops a new ambiguity for Fielding in *Amelia*. Miss Matthews, too violent to manipulate others, hears a rumor that James has killed Booth, relents toward Booth, feels a return of passion for him, and busily manipulates her own feelings: she "looked on James as the tool with which she had done this murder . . . as it is usual for people who have rashly or inadvertently made any animate or inanimate thing the instrument of mischief to hate the innocent means by which the mischief was effected (for this is a subtle method which the mind invents to excuse ourselves, the last objects on whom we would willingly wreak our vengeance)" (V, viii). Miss Matthews is thus a more serious and pathological version of the passion-dominated and therefore self-deluding Lady Booby.

Such delusion, as in the earlier novels, is manifestly both foolish and vicious self-enclosure. But in *Amelia* virtuous self-enclosure is sometimes approved with a sobriety previously uncharacteristic of the creator of Abraham Adams. Amelia's delusion about the relations between Booth and James is good: "So happily, both for herself and Mr. Booth, did the excellence of this good woman's disposition deceive her, and force her to see every thing in the most advantageous light to her husband" (IV, vi). Where technical madness of this sort had been explicitly ridiculed in Adams and Western and condemned in Lady Booby and the Man of the Hill and Thwackum, it is on the whole encouraged in Amelia. The approval is not revolutionary with Fielding; the regular retreat of his heroes to the country implies continuous pressure in the author supporting withdrawal. But never before was it so explicit as in the last, sad novel. In *Amelia*, Fielding has moved a good way from *Don Quixote* in the direction of *The Iceman Cometh*.

The high point of the novel, its central section, is the attempt of the nameless lord to seduce Amelia, which is appropriately concentrated in the metaphor of the masquerade. But Lady Bellaston had told Tom that everyone at a masquerade knows everyone else, so that such an entertainment becomes a hopeless conscious device of self-delusion, relieved only by the presence of innocents like Tom and Amelia. The actual ball with which we are presented contains the central sermon by Dr. Harrison, whose wish to eradicate adultery is shown as useless crying in the wilderness; a sequence in which two disguised women (Mrs. James and Miss Matthews) vainly lecture Colonel James on his sins; and a trick by which Mrs. Atkinson pretends to be Amelia, deviously helping both Amelia and herself. At the Upton inn, high-spirited farce had revealed the harmless self-centeredness of most of the characters; in this climactic descent into hell, all motives but Amelia's and Booth's are shoddy, manipulative, devious. The stakes are mean— military promotion, prestige at the expense of others, sexuality without a trace of exuberance—and the game is wearying. Any reminder of virtue is a roaring joke. We are approaching the very modern world of *The Waste Land* and *No Exit*.

Much of Mrs. Atkinson's story—like the Man of the Hill's, an alternative for the title character's—relates to the theme of self-enclosure. When she describes the effect of her mother's death, her narrative is so stirring that Amelia nearly faints, an interaction creditable both to the emotions the narrator has felt and to those which affect the hearer. One has been able to break through ordinary falsities to communicate, and the other has been receptive (as Tom had responded to Mrs. Miller's account of the Andersons). Mrs. Atkinson's lapse was, characteristically, conditioned by her willing delusion, abetted by the lord's manipulation of it.

When she was living at Mrs. Ellison's, she met him and was delighted by his praise of her family, "foolishly considering, that
others saw with my eyes, and felt with my heart" (VII, vi). Amelia,
like Sophia, is too alert to the full identities of others for such
delusions.

Colonel James, so important in his effect on the Booths, is Fielding's most complex attempt to draw a self-enclosed figure realis-
tically. The complexity derives from the combination of ingredients: social and therefore political power, an indifferent disposition
overlaid by good manners and much distorted by selfish passion, and a corrupt society. James, "though a very generous man,
had not the least grain of tenderness in his disposition. His mind
was formed of those firm materials of which nature formerly
hammered out the Stoic, and upon which the sorrows of no man
living could make an impression." Such a man, says Fielding, will
do all sorts of things for the man he calls friend, unless the "favorite passion interposes," in which case he is unconcerned;
"Whereas the man whose tender disposition really feels the
miseries of another will endeavor to relieve them for his own
sake; and in such a mind friendship will often get the superiority
over every other passion" (VIII, v). The colonel's kindness is social and aloofly rational—he is rich enough to lend money carelessly and idle enough to spend time with Booth in the hospital—
but not personal, since his friends' joys and sorrows are not directly communicated to him. Nothing that does not minister to his
lust and vanity can penetrate his enclosure.

Through James also Fielding can argue his favorite doctrine
that people can understand in others only their own motivations.
The idea that Atkinson would willingly be his pimp with Amelia
for the sake of future military rewards came to him naturally:
"the colonel borrowed it from the knowledge of his own heart.
This dictated to him that he, from a bad motive, was capable of
desiring to debauch his friend's wife; and the same heart inspired
him to hope that another, from another bad motive, might be
guilty of the same breach of friendship in assisting him" (VIII,
viii). As in *Tom Jones,* the same psychology explains why good
people are less likely to be prudent than bad ones: guilt often
discovers the snares in its way, since it is alertly prying everywhere
to lay snares for others, "Whereas innocence, having no such purpose, walks fearlessly and carelessly through life, and is conse-

quently liable to tread on the gins which cunning hath laid to entrap it . . . it is not want of sense, but want of suspicion, by which innocence is often betrayed" (VIII, ix). Suspicion, Fielding goes on to say on this ambiguous subject, "is the great optic glass helping us to discern plainly almost all that passes in the minds of others, without some use of which nothing is more purblind than human nature" (IX, ii).

While Fielding had been saying the same thing as far back as the "Essay on the Knowledge of the Characters of Men," not before *Amelia* had he shown so clearly the normal danger to the good. Aside from the material danger—that James might destroy the future security of the Booths if Amelia resists his lust—James presents the subtler danger of causing Amelia to act deviously and therefore corruptly. To prevent Booth's learning of his advances and the duel which would inevitably ensue, she "was forced to act in a manner which she was conscious must give encouragement to the colonel; a situation which perhaps requires as great prudence and delicacy as any in which the heroic part of the female character can be exerted" (IX, ii). To cope with these complications, which even Dr. Harrison misunderstands, Amelia has to allow Mrs. Bennet to impersonate her at the ball. Since Mrs. Bennet has already been tainted, Fielding can have her take the initiative in this crime against communication. Where Tom Jones's insincere proposal to Lady Bellaston had caused him great difficulties, in the corrupt world of *Amelia* no virtue can survive without at least a minimal compromise, and the heroine's qualms are light. As much as in the first two novels, delusion, manipulation, and illusion are staples of human intercourse. But where Fielding had earlier insisted on the truth as firmly as Ibsen's Norah, he now must support some delusion and, even where the movers are such paragons as Amelia and Harrison, a measure of manipulation. Partly, this is greater melancholy of vision; partly, greater realism in technique. For Fielding, the two were inevitably united.

As I have suggested earlier, sex is a major medium by which Fielding symbolically demonstrates both morality and psychology. In each of the novels, the completely communicative love of the hero and heroine is contrasted, in the framework and details of the action, with the self-enclosed lusts of others. All of the heroes are given opportunities to make sexual conveniences of willing women in sequences on which the plots of the novels turn. All the heroines are the objects of male lust.

In *Joseph Andrews*, Lady Booby's appetite for Joseph, which is complicated by her high-bred neuroses, is largely mental, made up of fantasies of his beauty and nourished by scandals of the lovers of great ladies. While Mrs. Slipslop's tigerish lust is completely animal, expressing itself in treats of food and drink, Lady Booby intellectually assumes that social conventions are on her side, and is shocked when Joseph speaks to her of preserving his virtue. Though this is supposed to be and is hilarious, it nonetheless re-affirms Joseph's insistence on his individual humanity and forces Lady Booby, toward the end of the book, to think of him as a person rather than as a generic handsome footman from whom his mistress can fairly demand sexual adventure. Though Lady Booby is not sensitive to the purport of his arguments, a good deal of her later perplexity is caused by Joseph's popping out from anonymity to personality.

Fanny's attractions, which Fielding describes in gastronomical terms, arouse in various men the sexual hunger that at times forms the basis of the plot. She enters the novel on the edge of rape, where Fielding balances her, sometimes pathetically and always absurdly, through encounters with the vicious roasting squire, Didapper's servant, and minor dangers like the justices before whom she appears. So obviously is she a symbol of sexual convenience to surrounding society that Beau Didapper, plainly effeminate, tries to use her as a device by which to assert manly potency. And so powerful and mysterious is beauty for Fielding at this stage that even Abraham Adams, in Lady Booby's enchanted castle, finds himself magically in bed with her. At the end, sexual activity is directly and amusingly contrasted to the central message of Christianity: Adams's sermon to the assembled company "concluded with strongly asserting that there was no such thing as pleasure in this [world]. At which Pamela and her husband smiled on one another" (IV, xiii).

But the relations among the central trio are completely opposite to such self-enclosure. While Joseph and Fanny both seek the pleasure of sex (which is neutral rather than bad), they are willing to subordinate their desires to social law, to the church's codification of divine law, and, above all, to the loving guidance of Adams. In all of Joseph's rescues of Fanny it is her welfare he is centrally concerned with, and when Fanny heard that Joseph was sick at an inn, she "that instant abandoned the cow she was milking" and went off to find him (II, x). Though Adams is less divorced from this world than he would admit—witness his vanity and his earthly concern for his child—in his responsiveness to the needs of all people he shows a deeper outgoing love than his final sermon suggests.

In *Tom Jones,* Fielding even more specifically and significantly makes sex an element of the central themes and structure. Formally, the introductory chapter of Book VI discusses both the nature of love, a force urging us outside ourselves, and the ways in which our own minds determine whether we can or cannot see objects of love. The implications of the first novel—often ambiguous, as in the relations of Joseph and Fanny—are here developed in an explicit theory. Those philosophers who claim that God, love, and virtue in human nature do not exist, Fielding says, have used the same method as the goldfinders, "viz., the searching, rummaging, and examining into a nasty place; indeed, in the former instances, into the nastiest of all places, A BAD MIND." "The truth-finder, having raked out that jakes, his own mind, and being there capable of tracing no ray of divinity, nor anything virtuous or good, or lovely, or loving, very fairly, honestly, and logically concludes that no such things exist in the whole creation." Fielding then lists the ways in which love can affect us: 1) "many minds, and perhaps those of the philosophers, are entirely free from the least traces of such a passion"; 2) lust is more properly hunger than love; 3) "this love for which I am an advocate, though it satisfies itself in a much more delicate manner, doth nevertheless seek its own satisfaction as much as the grossest of all our appetites"; 4) when directed toward one of the other sex, love uses this hunger for complete satisfaction, and it heightens the delights of the hunger "to a degree scarce imaginable by those who have never been susceptible of any other emotions than what have proceeded from appetite alone" (VI, i).

The source of love is outgoing benevolence. Having granted various concessions to the Mandevillians, Fielding wants in return an agreement "that there is in some (I believe in many) human breasts a kind and benevolent disposition which is gratified by contributing to the happiness of others. That in this gratification alone, as in friendship, in parental and filial affection, as indeed in general philanthropy, there is a great and exquisite delight" (VI, i). Such pleasure may be heightened by sexual love, but may exist without it. But this outgoing benevolence is particularly spurred by a stimulus from without (the essential idea, that if men can recognize the good they eagerly seek it, going back to the Greeks). "Lastly, that esteem and gratitude are the proper motives to love, as youth and beauty are to desire, and, therefore, though such desire may naturally cease, when age or sickness overtakes its object, yet these can have no effect on love, nor ever shake or remove, from a good mind, that sensation or passion which hath gratitude and esteem for its basis" (VI, i).

The distinction between sex and love, as here defined, becomes a device by which Fielding can show the difference between morality as it is and as it should be, and between innocence and experience. For example, he elaborately contrasts the love of a young girl with that of a woman like Bridget, whose concupiscence had led to a basic plot complication of the novel, the question of Tom's parentage. The girl is unsure, bashful, and affected by the appearance of beauty in figure and dress, while the older woman is aware of herself, assured, interested mainly in whether the man's strength promises frequent sexual pleasures. Innocence yields, is able to go out of itself; experience, at least in this area, leads to increased use of the partner for one's own purposes. Partridge's aggressive wife can be consoled in bed for her jealousy over Jenny, so that her unjustified scolding ends in her receiving personal pleasure (the principle is the same as with the Towwouses of the first novel, though Partridge had not been unfaithful). Youth does not mean inexperience, as Molly Seagrim's involvements with Square and the country Lothario show; however, Fielding points out that her youth has made her more engagingly vulnerable, less able to manipulate sex for her own advantage, than older practitioners like Mrs. Waters and Lady Bellaston.

At the end, Tom insists that through all his superficial affairs, for which he blames the grossness of male sexuality, he has loved only Sophia. Though Fielding has shown Tom as frankly delighted by animal pleasure, he has never permitted him to be manipulative. Even the involvement with Lady Bellaston had come from Tom's compliant, affectionate disposition, a specific contrast to her mercenary wish to buy sex. Tom accepts her money as given in the same spirit as his kindly response to her, not as payment but as a testimonial of good will. To make sure that we understand Tom's views, Fielding has him reject a proposal of marriage made by a rich and unexceptionable widow at a time when he is destitute and has little hope of marrying Sophia. For Tom, we are to understand, sex is purely the most pleasant medium for the expression of his immense good will. Essentially, Tom acts out Fielding's definition of love at all times, in degrees varying from total benevolent sympathy toward Sophia, through lesser stages declining from Molly to casual responsiveness to Lady Bellaston.

The central action of *Amelia* is two-fold, involving Booth's attempt to resist temptation and establish himself and the attempts by every man in London to sleep with Amelia. Booth, representing good nature with no prudence whatever, must fail without Harrison's help, an easy victim of seduction or duplicity. His fundamental difficulty is in the unsuitability of his own character for a corrupt and encroaching society. The only solutions are religion and escape. But Amelia, who has all the circumspection natural to her serene and temperate mind, is persecuted by others. She is in no way at fault.

However, her very perfection is an ideal goal which in part excuses her pursuers. Colonel James, Fielding says, was not wholly to blame for desiring Amelia: "I am firmly persuaded that to withdraw admiration from exquisite beauty, or to feel no delight in gazing at it, is as impossible as to feel no warmth from the most scorching rays of the sun. To run away is all that is in our power" (VI, i).[3] Beauty is thus a sort of emanation, an excursive power, a visual and imaginative stimulus to the self-pleasing passions of others which can also call forth any good will they may have. For this reason, Fielding came to see sexual love as our most dangerous passion. It is the strongest mechanism for taking us out of ourselves, but it is at least partly self-interested and, like all passions, prevents our clear perception of reality: "what is worst of all, there is [no other passion] to whose poison and infatuation the best of minds are so liable . . . not only tenderness and good nature, but bravery, generosity, and every virtue are often made the instruments of effecting the most atrocious purposes of this all-subduing tyrant" (VI, i).

In contrast, when the sexual passion is united with a completely outward concern for another, as it is in Amelia's feeling for Booth and in Atkinson's for Amelia, it leads to noble selflessness. And the person who can love in this way becomes himself intensely lovable. Mrs. Bennet marries Atkinson because of his attitude toward Amelia (as Miss Matthews had fallen in love with Booth because he adored Amelia): "In short, I have discovered he hath always loved you with such a faithful, honest, noble, generous passion, that I was consequently convinced his mind must possess all the ingredients of such a passion; and what are these but true honor, goodness, modesty, bravery, tenderness, and, in a word, every human virtue" (VII, x). Even the less worthy women, who are themselves unable to feel or to arouse intense love, keep trying to achieve it vicariously. They have enough sense of the existence of others to understand the value of love, though they cannot feel it.

In sexual relations, then, Fielding concentrates most clearly his vision of the ways in which good and bad minds react to individual human beings, who after all constitute their social context. Like many a modern novelist, he sees sexual attraction as a particularly direct method of initiating love, which is the most intense sense of the existence of others. In sexual love one of the strongest self-satisfying passions is combined with the strongest emanation of goodness toward another. However, sex is also the most convenient avenue by which a badly disposed or indifferent person may turn others into machines for his own pleasures, and for this reason Fielding often uses it to show brutality, meanness, and prideful disdain. As with professions of devotion to all the other ideals, the only sure criterion of virtue in love is motivation; and motivation is barely discernible.

From the beginning to the end of Fielding's career, from the plays and *Shamela* to *Amelia*, he insisted on the distinction between an intensified disposition to act kindly to another (and in the process become sublimely happy oneself), which was love, and the tendency to use another for one's sensual gratification, which he saw as the widespread corruption of love. Justice Squeezum, Wild, Blifil, and the lord in *Amelia*, as well as all the lecherous women like Lady Raffler, Tishy Snap, Lady Booby, Lady Bellaston, and Miss Matthews, stand therefore in contrast to real lovers like Parson Adams, Joseph, Fanny, Tom, Sophia, Amelia, Booth, and Atkinson, whose love is a benevolent disposition leading out of the self. In between are the goodnaturedly helpless, who combine yielding dispositions with some selfish desires for pleasure coming from almost any attractive source—Betty the chambermaid, Doshy Snap, Jenny Jones, Mrs. Fitzpatrick, and perhaps even Mrs. Bennet. The good reach out of themselves, consciously wishing the good of another in love, and in turn feel the most glowing sense of happiness within themselves. The bad, concerned only with the satisfaction of their desires, remain imprisoned while they gorge themselves. The rest—the largest number—dimly perceive the desire and the other person, achieving some satisfaction and much mental confusion.

Another problem involving the relationship of inward and outward, the degree to which the well-disposed innocent must curb his disposition and protect himself against society—i.e., the issue of prudence—has been often discussed, but not from the viewpoint of the present study. Parson Adams' complex effect is derived partially from the ambiguity inherent in this issue: he is "entirely ignorant" of the way of the world in situations so clear-cut that we tend to join the world in laughing at him before we realize that he is morally right. Joseph, on the other hand, while innocent enough to be good and attractive, stops this side of simple-mindedness: he had understood Lady Booby's intentions, Fielding informs us, for otherwise he "would not have had an understanding sufficient for the principal subject of such a book as this" (I, x).

The words are written in jest, but for Fielding the problem, whether perceptiveness is a necessary constituent of value in character, is not simple. Where Jane Austen, for example, saw intelligence and clarity of vision as absolutely essential to the complex character, which she valued above the simple one even when the pure "goodness" of the latter is perhaps greater (her preference for Elizabeth Bennet over Jane)[4] and where even Richardson saw intelligence as central to maturity, Fielding usually finds goodness alone sufficient. His admirable characters are not required to have any rational understanding of the nature of others, at least before *Amelia*. It is even sometimes a merit in them not to recognize evil, since his epistemology makes them unable to recognize qualities unlike their own. Consequently, his models of virtue, like Adams, Allworthy, and Harrison, are easily imposed on by much grosser personalities, where Elizabeth Bennet can only be fooled by the ambiguities of Wickham, and Clarissa Harlowe

faces in Lovelace a monster of perverse intelligence. Suspiciousness, which Richardson sees as a necessary virtue, is for Fielding
(as for Melville) bad in itself. He bemoans the need for the modi-
cum of worldly wisdom which would prevent his virtuous characters from being destroyed, and he either arranges for his villains
to make transparent mistakes of which a Lovelace would never be
guilty or provides convenient dei ex machina at crises to save his
innocents. Fielding shows us a much simpler split between good
and evil (despite occasional assurances that we all have the "seeds"
of both within us) and is, in this respect, much more consistently
sentimental than Richardson, Jane Austen, or even Sterne.

A well-known dialogue between Tow-wouse and his wife illustrates the problem of prudence as Fielding sees it. Moved by the
plight of Joseph, Tow-wouse urges on Mrs. Tow-wouse the claims
of common charity. Her answer is that "common charity teaches
us to provide for ourselves, and our families" (I, xii). Ironically
presented, here is Fielding's persistent conflict, unavoidable in a
marred society, between charity and prudence. Unquestionably,
at times dogmatically, he argues for the primacy of the first; but
he is forced by the evils of society and widespread selfishness to
counsel his virtuous characters and readers to defend themselves
with the second. We are to despise Parson Trulliber for telling
Adams, who has been preaching charity, that "I know what charity
is, better than to give to vagabonds" (II, xiv); but we are to admire
the caution of Wilson, who is suspicious of a clergyman, a footman, and a pretty girl wandering to his house at night: he "knew
too much of the world to give a hasty belief to professions" (III,
ii). Without a key to character—which good nature cannot give
us—in *Joseph Andrews* we can only hope to retreat, like Wilson
and Joseph, to estates in the country where our innocent trust will
be safe.

In *Joseph Andrews,* prudence is attributed largely to unattrac-
tive characters, though its absence is no guarantee of virtue. The
prudent ones are Mrs. Tow-wouse, the people in the coach (especially the lawyer), Peter Pounce the usurious steward, Lawyer
Scout, the vicious squire's toadies, a variety of minor figures, and
(though her hard life may excuse her) Mrs. Adams, who "was one
of those prudent people who never do anything to injure their
families, or perhaps one of those good mothers who would even
stretch their conscience to serve their children" (IV, viii). Con-

spicuous among the imprudent are Adams, the early Wilson, Fanny, and Joseph: had he prudently made a sexual convenience of Lady Booby, his fortune would have been made; following the steps of his prudent sister, he might even have married the lady. However, it is also true that Lady Booby and the vicious squire are imprudent, because of the uncontrolled violence of their passions. Evidently, prudence is a mechanism for the limitation of the passions. When it is dominant, it is suspect as an agent for selfish defense against others; when it is completely absent, the self is revealed naked, good or bad, to the world.

Tom Jones plays a good many variations on this theme. A central subject is Tom's education, his need to learn prudence, his learning it, and his good fortune in being able to enjoy its fruits. With deliberate ambiguity, the argument is vitiated by the events themselves, since no amount of prudence could have gotten him Sophia without the fortuitous discovery of his parentage, and since his opposite number is shown as a model of evil prudence. If Tom's character had been otherwise, he would not have gotten into trouble; but then he would not have been much worth saving.

The contemptible Blifil and the blameless Allworthy are the two exemplars of prudence in the novel. Blifil, we are told early, was "a lad of a remarkable disposition; sober, discreet, and pious beyond his age" (III, ii). But not long afterward Fielding gives a partly ironic direction to "my young readers": "goodness of heart and openness of temper, though these may give them greater comfort within, and administer to an honest pride in their own minds, will by no means, alas! do their business in the world. Prudence and circumspection are necessary even to the best of men. They are indeed, as it were, a guard to Virtue, without which she can never be safe. It is not enough that your designs, nay, that your actions, are intrinsically good; you must take care that they shall appear so"; "no man can be good enough to enable him to neglect the rules of prudence" (III, vii). Well and good—but only three pages later, so close that we cannot imagine Fielding's ignorance of the juxtaposition,[5] Blifil is shown buying Tom's Bible for half price (Tom wanted the money to provide food for the Seagrim family), "for he was a very prudent lad, and so careful of his money that he had laid up almost every penny which he had received from Mr. Allworthy" (III, ix). As Fielding often shows, and sometimes says, for Blifil prudence is partly a manipulative device and partly a mechanical substitute for passion.

Thinking himself on his death-bed, Allworthy tells Tom, in a passage cited by everyone who has discussed the novel, "I am convinced, my child, that you have much goodness, generosity, and honor in your temper; if you will add prudence and religion to these, you must be happy; for the three former qualities, I admit, make you worthy of happiness, but they are the latter only which will put you in possession of it" (V, vii). This is the formal thesis of the book; but it would hold up less ambiguously if Allworthy were not so consistently imposed on by appearances and by ill-disposed people. A better case is made for prudence (which is, however, implied, not specifically mentioned) in Fielding's famous discussion of the wise man's careful purchasing of all pleasures in this world's market, without paying too dearly for any.

The last novel is ostensibly concerned with the same issue, though any reader can see that without help Booth is doomed, prudent or imprudent. At any rate, Fielding here faces the problem of determinism and prudence, at least in his exordium: "I question much whether we may not, by natural means, account for the success of knaves, the calamities of fools, with all the miseries in which men of sense sometimes involve themselves, by quitting the directions of Prudence, and following the blind guidance of a predominant passion; in short, for all the ordinary phenomena which are imputed to fortune, whom, perhaps, men accuse with no less absurdity in life than a bad player complains of ill luck at the game of chess" (I, i). Chance and a predominant passion can both be overcome by prudence, assuming that we can make rational choices of this sort. Some distance into the novel, Fielding again makes clear that prudence is a social virtue, not an absolute one, and that it is forced on anyone who wishes to survive in society: "As the malicious disposition of mankind is too well known, and the cruel pleasure which they take in destroying the reputations of others, the use we are to make of this knowledge is to afford no handle to reproach" (III, i). At this stage, Fielding directly argues for prudence, but he seems unable to persuade himself or Booth or us that we can alter our characters voluntarily. In a world where buying a modest coach causes an industrious man's neighbors to ruin him and where helping a weak man fight off thugs leads to imprisonment, prudence would counsel the sort of stolid inactivity that Fielding everywhere finds hateful.

Virtuous women, it appears, form a special subdivision within the generally ambiguous class of prudent people. Sophia, for example, is prudent though virtuous, young, inexperienced, and spontaneously delightful. In her and in Amelia, Fielding seems to be suggesting that good and intelligent women, by nature or social pressure, are inevitably more prudent than men. Since their sphere of action should normally be limited to the family and perhaps the local poor, and since society early teaches them the need for defense, they evidently serve as repositories of virtue rather than as active agents. Like the well-ordered mind, they can inspire men to virtuous actions and respond to these with approval. Though Fielding never formulates such a distinction between the moral roles of men and women, it seems to me implicit in his view of their relations. The ideal woman—Sophia or Amelia—is by her very nature temperate and harmonious. Her prudence is thus not self-seeking caution, but a perception of disharmony in circumstances or people around her.

But what one is to conclude from Fielding's many references to prudence is not at all clear, except that most good people will inevitably be imprudent out of their eagerness to get outside themselves, and therefore we must be tolerant of their lapses and teach them to improve. This, according to Fielding's dedication to Lyttelton, was the moral aim of *Tom Jones:* "I have endeavoured strongly to inculcate, that virtue and innocence can scarce ever be injured but by indiscretion; and that it is this alone which often betrays them into the snares that deceit and villainy spread for them. A moral which I have the more industriously laboured, as the teaching it is, of all others, the likeliest to be attended with success; since, I believe, it is much easier to make good men wise, than to make bad men good." Good men need to develop prudence, as they need to use their reason and their senses, to help them perceive the nature of surrounding reality as clearly as possible. But unless prudence is an instrument at the disposal of religion and the virtues with which Allworthy has credited Tom, it is likely to affect the center of character rather than appear on the perimeter. A passion for prudence is rather like a passion for a club or a gun. Conspicuous prudence proclaims the person at war.

Certain moral implications of the inward-outward paradox, implicit in what I have been saying, should be spelled out. The most important, as is evident from Fielding's discussions of love and of greatness, is that the perceived humanity of others forms the basis of sympathy and therefore of charity. In general, the virtuous people in the first novel are those who can feel for others; or rather, Fanny and Joseph can feel directly for others, while Adams is devoted to abstract principles of charity which may or may not fit practical situations. Adams can respond with capers of delight to the love of the two young people, but he may be insulated by the ideal religious and moral world which his mind has constructed: note the contrast between his responses to the news of his son's drowning and to the reputed sibling relationship of the lovers. All the bad characters and most of the neutral ones (like the passengers in the coach) are prevented by concern for self from sympathizing with others, while Adams's fundamental absurdity (and integrity) derives from the occasional conflict between his hugely good disposition and his equally extreme devotion to principle. Unlike the bad, who rationalize selfishness with the saws of prudence, he is as free from selfishness as a man can be; he is absolutely indifferent to his own welfare in the world. Where principle does not interfere, he can feel directly for everyone, including even the characters in the story of Leonora. Where he seems insensitive, as in his lecture to Joseph while they are helpless to save Fanny from rape, Fielding is demonstrating the impossibility of any consolation, whether from reason or from religion, in the extreme of distress. What Adams says then is most sensible; but reason cannot still emotions so intense, which only a lover in the same circumstances can feel. While Adams serves to warn us of the useless weltering in feeling which was to characterize later novels of sentiment, our sympathy is with Joseph. As the absurdity of Adams suggests, for Fielding the ideal of morality is not the uncompromising wayfaring Christian but the less theological post-Lockean who can leave the self to feel with others.

While this is Fielding's attitude all through the first novel, he does not seem to me to use it as a structurally unifying theme; not until *Tom Jones* is he capable of pointing all the forces of the novel toward a positive moral end. And at least one important aspect of this end, if not its central aspect, involves the ideal of moral contentment within the self, deriving from the ability to feel for others, to leave the self to act for them, and to return happy.

Abraham Adams had defined charity as "a generous disposition to relieve the distressed" (III, xiii); in Tom Jones this disposition is more elaborately conceived as a faculty to bring him into participation in the mental states of others. Tom has a quality which, Fielding says, while its name is not uniformly agreed on, "doth certainly inhabit some human breasts; whose use is not so properly to distinguish right from wrong as to prompt and incite them to the former, and to restrain and withhold them from the latter" (IV, vi). Some people are concerned only with themselves, regarding the welfare of others as irrelevant; but "there is a different temper of mind which borrows a degree of virtue even from self-love. Such can never receive any kind of satisfaction from another, without loving the creature to whom that satisfaction is owing, and without making its well-being in some sort necessary to their own ease" (IV, vi). Tom's love for Molly, the unconscious responsiveness of the good man, is of this sort. Furthermore, since Tom automatically communicates harmless good will to those who share this quality, others' opinions of Tom are major criteria of their own virtue:[6] the seeds of goodness in the highwayman, Nightingale, Jenny Waters, even Mrs. Fitzpatrick and various landladies when their self-interest is not involved, even the wilfully enclosed Man of the Hill, all thrive like Jack's beans when Tom shines upon them.

All of Fielding's heroes emanate a challenge to good will, and the nature of others has a chance to respond. While Adams is too crotchety to arouse this response except from his charges, Joseph inspires it in varieties of people: the postilion, Betty the chambermaid, even Lady Booby and Slipslop in their hunger for his beauty. Similarly, Amelia to a considerable extent and Booth to a slighter one arouse outgoing goodness in people who little suspect their own capacities. The theme, which may simply derive from Fielding's lasting sympathy for youth, beauty, and high spirits, is everywhere the celebration of that inward faculty of loving of which Tom is the embodiment.

In *Amelia* Fielding uses the novel form as a means of expressing through his creatures the theories of virtuous communication about which he had previously sermonized. That is, *Joseph Andrews* and *Tom Jones* are primarily rational demonstrations and appeals; comedy is, traditionally, rational. Fielding makes quite sure that the absurdity of Adams stands between Joseph's lamentations for his acutely endangered beloved and us. In Sophia's similar distress, Western bursts in hallooing and swearing, dissipating the tension in laughter. But in *Amelia,* which is determinedly serious (compare, for example, the relatively rounded and restrained treatment of Colonel Bath with that of his prototype, Squire Western), the appeal is directly to the fellow-feeling of the reader. We are to be distressed with Amelia when she thinks Booth has been deliberately unfaithful, or when she has to decide about the masquerade; with Booth, when he wastes the money needed for sustenance. As in the sentimental literature of the time generally, the feeling response is the goal. Fielding has not abandoned intellectual communication completely—he has not gone so far as Sterne, for whom words merely obstruct communication—but he is convinced of the didactic superiority of what he conceives to be Richardson's method.

But even if goodness is an effluence of the disposition, not dependent on intellect, in the most effective people reason, or prudence, or judgment must be operative, so that the goodness will not be wasted or invite destruction. In a world where many wear masks, where communication is therefore very hard, the success of virtue will be commensurate with the good man's understanding of the motives of others. But such understanding is hard to achieve. We must always consider that what might be our motives for an action are not necessarily those of someone else, unless, through intimacy, we know that person to be like ourselves. Since the world is a complicated and distorted place, where actions often go astray, Fielding says, through Heartfree, that motivation alone can be morally judged—what was in the mind of the actor, not necessarily what form his action took or what consequence it had. The good mistake the motives of the evil, and the evil mistake those of the good; but the good can feel more than the evil, have a much wider range of emotions, and therefore even if they mistake, their goodness still receives its internal reward.

The attempt to determine motives and to apportion suitable rewards and punishments forms a significant element in the novels. In *Joseph Andrews,* motives are fairly transparent. In most situations where ambiguity would be possible, as in Lady Booby's motives when she attempts to seduce Joseph, Fielding takes us directly into the minds of the characters to observe their conflict-ing passions. But at least once he uses the technique which was to pervade the second novel. When Joseph lies groaning in the ditch, and the good-natured postilion has drawn the attention of the pas-sengers to him, the lawyer persuades the others to pick him up. This might seem an act of pure charity; but neither the lawyer nor the others, as samples of ordinary human nature, are very charitable. Consequently, the lawyer is made to reveal his under-lying motivation, with which the others are in sympathy: Joseph might die in the ditch, and then they, as the last people to notice him, would be responsible. Lest we should think that motives are less important than actions in determining morality, Fielding later lectures us on the exemplary selfishness of the lawyer.

Tom Jones, which claims to serve up human nature in all its variety, focuses more on the difficulty of determining motivation than its predecessor. At one point, Fielding even deliberately pro-vides a motiveless and meaningless act to prove how hard it is to read minds. Blifil, seeing a girl sinking to the ground with Tom, informs Thwackum but does not identify Tom: "why he did so must be left to the judgment of the sagacious reader; for we never choose to assign motives to the actions of men, when there is any possibility of our being mistaken" (V, x). However, no novelist professing to describe human nature and to teach how to live in a confusing world can make such actions frequent. Fielding is say-ing, like Locke, that one cannot be certain of motivation in any one act. But he also says that from observing the pattern of ac-tions of a person we may deduce his motivation. In his show-piece analysis of Black George's mind when George considers stealing Tom's money, Fielding reminds us to look for this pattern: "A single bad act no more constitutes a villain in life than a single bad part on the stage. The passions, like the managers of a play-house, often force men upon parts without consulting their judg-ment, and sometimes without any regard to their talents" (VII, i). We can never be certain about motivation, but we can have a pretty accurate idea if we have frequently observed the actions of others and examined their alternatives.

Dr. Blifil, for example, showed "a great appearance of religion. Whether his religion was real, or consisted only in appearance, I shall not presume to say, as I am not possessed of any touchstone which can distinguish the true from the false" (I, x). (As a matter of technique, Fielding raises the question only when the answer is foregone.) Captain Blifil mistreated his brother after the marriage, causing Fielding to speculate on the devil's principle of kicking your friends after you have risen by their help: "Whether the captain acted by this maxim, I will not positively determine; so far we may confidently say, that his actions may be fairly derived from this diabolical principle" (I, xiii). As the showman and not the inventor of Vanity Fair, and as a good Lockean, Fielding can only estimate motive from the pattern of action. As an ironic voice, he can underline for us the difference between action and professed motivation.

Square is another whom the narrator, as a guide to human nature, is forced to assess obliquely. He thought "all virtue a matter of theory only. This, it is true, he never affirmed . . . ; and yet upon the least attention to his conduct, I cannot help thinking it was his real opinion, as it will perfectly reconcile some contradictions which might otherwise appear in his character" (III, iii). Sophia's mind is so wonderful, Fielding informs the reader, that he will barely describe it: "nay, it is a kind of tacit affront to our reader's understanding, and may also rob him of that pleasure which he will receive in forming his own judgment of her character" (IV, ii). Very often, the effect of claiming to know intimately the minds of the good people and not of the bad is to align the narrator and his readers with the virtuous, who seek their way in a world which is bent on misleading them.

The sequence of events of the day on which Allworthy was believed to be dying is a special illustration of the problem of determining the true attitude of others when one's own vanity or their hypocrisy has caused major distortions. At the announcement of Allworthy's will, Thwackum's and Square's discontent is not stated, but it can be gauged from their countenances and from the dialogue between them. Thwackum, a sincere victim of his own delusive vanity, is even certain of the damnation of Allworthy, whom we know to be destined for heaven. Similarly, Square and Mrs. Wilkins show the selfish motives underlying their service to the squire, as well as their false assumption of his stupidity on the basis of his consistent acceptance of their surface professions. Allworthy's misjudgment of Tom, on the other hand, is a legitimate response, supported by the objective evidence of Tom's incautious acts, to what has been presented as reality.

Where none of the characters can be sure of others' motivations, the corrupt have misjudged because of their internal natures. The virtuous man has also misjudged, but only on the basis of a combination of damning events and deliberate distortions. When the distortions are removed and the virtuous pattern of Tom's life can be assessed, Allworthy gladly changes his judgment. Square, with enough goodness to recognize that he has not acted well, can reform on his deathbed. Thwackum, who is perfectly deluded and perfectly insulated against perceiving others' true motives, cannot change.

The problem of motivation pervades the novel, though Fielding more rarely after the first quarter or so speculates on individual motives, on the assumption that we are well enough acquainted with the behavioral patterns of the characters to do our own detecting. However, as both a practicing lawyer and an amateur psychologist, he remains interested in the problem of delusion and illusion as it affects the characters themselves. Mrs. Fitzpatrick, a good deal more credulous than Fielding and his instructed reader, and moreover partly deluding herself, explains her slowness to realize her husband's true nature: "women will suggest a thousand excuses to themselves for the folly of those they like; besides, . . . it requires a most penetrating eye to discern a fool through the disguises of gaiety and good breeding" (XI, v). On his simplified principles of the atomic constituents of motivation, Fielding explains that Honour's anger at a politicking landlord was caused by an insult to her prestige: "Thus the passion of Mrs. Honour appears natural enough, even if it were to be no otherwise accounted for; but, in reality, there was another cause of her anger" —she was roaring drunk (XI, viii).

When Allworthy has the evidence both of Tom's goodness and of Blifil's rascality before him, he makes the necessary generalization: "there is a great difference between those faults which candor may construe into imprudence, and those which can be deduced from villainy only." The former, he says, can ruin a man, but if he reforms, he can in time be respected; but villainy, when discovered, "is irretrievable" (XVIII, x). Here would seem to be a way out of the problem of motivation, but the practical difficulties are obvious: had Allworthy died before the discovery, no just conclusion would have been possible. Indeed, Fielding offers no real solution in *Tom Jones*, except that God cannot be fooled, and that the fruits of villainy are inevitably sour within the minds of the villains. So also are the fruits of imprudence, as witness Tom's mental condition when he thinks he has lost Sophia and committed manslaughter and incest. The result, demonstrated rather than stated, is a truism. We must use every mental and moral resource at our disposal with which to look out, to see the world clearly so that we may act well in it. We may still act wrongly, but the judges within our minds will absolve us.

Amelia, the most realistic of the novels, therefore has the most ambiguous characters to illustrate the complexity of human nature. Only the heroine is good and simple, presumably as evidence that such qualities are possible in a sordid world. Booth, the hero, is a sleazier version of Tom, weakly waiting for someone to give him a commission in the army, easily seducible by Miss Matthews, easily fooled into gambling with sharpers and losing the money which his family needed for subsistence; he is at the same time, like Tom, open-hearted, kind, brave, in most respects a manly fellow. Miss Matthews, though a whore, yet has occasional decent sentiments, is capable of considerable generosity, and gladly acts for the right in the rare situations when her passions are not involved against it. Mrs. Bennet is one of the good people, and yet it was partly her vanity which allowed the wholly evil lord to rape her; she advances her husband through duplicity, not caring if in the process she embarrasses Amelia; and she can be both envious and drunk. Mrs. Ellison, the procuress for her cousin, is again ambiguous. Despite her vicious practice, she is a kind landlady and a congenial neighbor. Furthermore, she gratuitously persuaded her cousin to settle a handsome pension on Mrs. Bennet after one sexual experience. The Jameses are ambiguous, and so is Colonel Bath. Human nature, *Amelia* demonstrates for Fielding, is too complicated for abstract formulation, particularly when it is examined in the context of real social and economic pressures.

The Jameses in *Amelia* are Fielding's most complex examples of the difficulty of understanding motivation. The colonel himself, as I have suggested, is explained by the combination of a neutral disposition—neither outgoing nor evil—with selfish vanity and lust, all set in a fairly high social stratum. Mrs. James is somewhat different. When she visits Amelia, she is quite cold: "And what was her present behavior more than that of a fine lady who considered form and show as essential ingredients of human happiness, and imagined all friendship to consist in ceremony, courtesies, messages, and visits" (IV, vi). At another stage, however, her behavior changes: "besides that of a fine lady, which is all mere art and mummery, every such woman hath some real character at the bottom, in which, whenever nature gets the better of her, she acts. Thus the finest ladies in the world will sometimes love, and sometimes scratch, according to the different natural dispositions, with great fury and violence, though both of these are equally inconsistent with a fine lady's artificial character" (VIII, ix). Mrs. James changes once or twice more, showing a basic neutrality like her husband's, being sometimes good natured, sometimes willing to lure Amelia to her husband in exchange for liberty to stay in town, sometimes mildly interested in seducing Booth. In general, despite the magnificent high-comedy scene between the Jameses (XI, i), their development is inconsistent and sometimes fumbling. For the first time in his fiction, Fielding is attempting with them and with Colonel Bath to show something of the changes which time and environment can make in characters constituted in certain ways; however, his simplified atomic psychology is inadequate to the experiment. Having abandoned comedy as his mode of seeing life, he has lost the detachment which would have made even sympathetic understanding of them possible. Thackeray did not make this mistake when, using *Amelia* as his base, he wrote *Vanity Fair*.

Motivation, regardless of the relative success with which he shows its effects, is for Fielding central in the assessment of human nature. It can derive from a variety of passions acting in different proportions, but, as Sherburn has noted, it is ultimately judged by its sources in indrawn selfishness or outgoing love (charity, expansiveness). The former leads to pain; the latter, to pleasure. Furthermore, selfishness for Fielding derives from pain, while charity may derive from either. That is, while the good man is pained by ills which he sees about him, his quality of goodness is absolute, seeking to move toward action even without what Locke had considered the stronger incentive. Even if Tom's pleased willingness to sleep with Mrs. Waters, or his eagerness to marry Sophia, may derive from the pain of not possessing them, his wish to do them good is a positive, not a negative quality. The pleasure it promises him is augmentation of the inward contentment with which he is already supplied.

The difficulties of disentangling motivation to discover the nature of human character verge on another problem pervasive in Fielding, that of detaching form from substance, of telling whether the form is an expression of the substance or is an affectation to fool the perceiver. Most conspicuously this problem involves religion, and most specifically the argument over faith and works. Fielding, as many have shown,[7] insisted that the essence of Christianity was charity, and that any attempt to preach a religion in which salvation depended on repression and election instead of on active charity was an encouragement to hypocrisy, if not in itself hypocritical. Barnabas, the curate where the badly mauled Joseph has been deposited, insists that faith is far superior to good works; and we find that though he is not an actively bad man, and does his duty to the letter even to the extent of attending on the spiritual health of a footman, his heart is really in gourmandising. Parson Trulliber, a much worse priest, is an even stronger propagandist for faith without works, and explains that he knows the meaning of charity too well to give to vagabonds like Adams.

As the early parts of *Tom Jones* make clear, charity is the chief criterion by which virtue can be judged in the absence of windows to people's minds. The novel opens with the contrast between Mrs. Wilkins' legalistic view that the bastard should be put at the churchwarden's door despite its danger from exposure, and Allworthy's immediate, charitable orders that its needs be met. Captain Blifil argues "that the word charity in Scripture nowhere means beneficence or generosity" (II, v) and insists on the superiority of faith to works. Allworthy answers that actually giving charity is a duty, as "let the word charity have what construction it would, it sufficiently appeared to be from the whole tenor of the New Testament" (II, v). Thwackum, who like every other objectionable priest in Fielding is convinced of innate depravity, "said in some instances what the world called charity appeared to him to be opposing the will of the Almighty, which had marked some particular persons for destruction" (III, viii). In general, Fielding sees charity as the essence of religion and morality: the act most symbolizing movement from within the enclosed self out to another. Where religion is used to support repression, or where it is not seen to center in charity, it is at best a lazy mouthing of clichés and more usually a mere mask for selfish motives.

The confusion of form and substance, illusion and reality, does not occur only in religion. It is pervasive wherever people mistake the world, either because they fool themselves or because they have been fooled by others. At times, it strikes us when a virtuous man innocently but devastatingly questions a system which seems to the rest of us self-evidently right. For example, Adams is shocked when he discovers that the bookseller with whom he discusses publishing his sermons will print anything that is likely to sell; Adams is certain that only morally useful works should be published, and we eventually wonder if he may not be right. When the decent lieutenant in *Tom Jones* insists that he believes both in Christianity and in the code of honor, ascribing inconsistencies to a bad translation of the Bible, our discovery is much less ambiguously directed. The opposition of reality and illusion is not very different from that suggested in a simile for the turmoil in Lady Booby's mind over whether to keep or dismiss Joseph: her mind was like a confused law case, "Or, as it happens in the conscience, where honour and honesty pull one way, and a bribe and necessity another" (I, ix). The law, like religion and like the idealized version of trade, is peculiarly available as a cloak for selfishness, being susceptible to mechanical use as an alternative to justice.

As we look over the novels, we find that the paradox of epistemological self-enclosure and the moral obligation of charity is everywhere important and sometimes central. Affectation, deriving from vanity and hypocrisy, is the general term for the process by which the self is denied knowledge of other selves outside it. Subjection to affectation strikingly involves the exploitation of others, who are seen as inferior beings, not people. In *Joseph Andrews,* knowledge of the outside world is almost totally limited to reflections of the characters' own experiences modified by their various degrees of vanity and affectation. Mr. Wilson and his family (in a modern Eden), the Joseph of the last three-fourths of the novel, and Fanny are the only characters not so modified. Within the psychological range of the novel, which Fielding says depends on affectation for its view of people, they are therefore the only figures without any special idiosyncratic qualities.

In *Tom Jones,* Fielding is more concerned to show the variety of ways in which people may be oriented by their idiosyncrasies to understand the world around them. Exhibiting the diversity of human character, he frequently argues that many people do not have certain passions or motivations, and therefore cannot recognize them in others. Some, like Blifil or Thwackum, cannot understand charity as a motive to action, because they lack any trace of it. For the same reason, some, like Tom, cannot at first recognize evil; and some, like the Man of the Hill, are so overwhelmed to discover malice that they are twisted far past a reasonable mental balance, seeing depravity everywhere where they had earlier not seen it at all.

No one can fully understand the worlds within and without. Not even the exemplary figures, such as Tom and Sophia, are able to see themselves with perfect objectivity. Like everyone else, they unconsciously edit their experiences to avoid even slight guilt, as witness the convenient omissions in their accounts of why they are loose on the road. Communication, except where the minds are similarly oriented, is therefore impossible. And the novel is so built that at its climax in Upton, self-enclosure is the dominant ingredient in motivation and plot, as self-enclosure is the key to the sensibility of the hermit whose story has just been told. Disinterestedness and experience, Fielding suggests, are the only qualities that can permit communication where identity of orientation is lacking; and the first is almost nonexistent when the self is involved. Sophia can suspect Mrs. Fitzpatrick's honesty because she herself is not affected; but Allworthy, though more experienced, fails to see through Blifil because of his own responsibility for the young man's upbringing. And while experience is essential, Fielding suggests, it can mean all things to all dispositions.

In *Amelia*, Fielding is more subtly concerned to show the distortions which the mind and its passions themselves create. Booth, a good person, has developed the bad device of blaming fate and chance for both his character and his treatment by the world. Arguing for submitting to one's character, delusions and all, he has abdicated the hard work of evaluating reality and dealing with it. Miss Matthews, a more credible Lady Booby, habitually works herself into love and hate. Inevitably, those most easily deluded are also most easily manipulated. Mrs. Bennet, more amenable to flattery than Amelia because her vanity is greater, is trapped into sexual exploitation by the lord, where Amelia overcomes more extended and varied attacks on her virtue. Susceptible to manipulation, Mrs. Bennet also manipulates, giving up the moral superiority which is normally the reward of the innocent, even the deceived innocent.

As is obvious to any reader, Fielding uses the orientation toward sex and love as a central criterion of the moral condition of his characters. Those who see sex as a device for making instruments of others to satisfy themselves—Lady Booby, Mrs. Slipslop, Lady Bellaston, Col. James, and the lord—have refused to come out of themselves. Those who love, the young couples in each novel, project good will toward the object of love, which then is augmented in its return to the self.

Love is one aspect of charity, Fielding's crucial virtue, and it is with charity that prudence must be contrasted throughout his novels. The moral goal is to be unreflectingly charitable by nature and yet not be mistreated by the world—and yet understand that evil exists and must be repudiated. Morally, spontaneous charity is always admirable, even where it is ignorant or foolish; but prudent actions depend for their status on the motivation of the agent. Whenever prudence conflicts with ideals, it should be summarily abandoned; leaders, for example, must never consider their own safety or advancement at the expense of their followers. Power over people, whether sexual, social, economic, or political, always presents the greatest moral danger to its possessors; since political power is most wide-ranging and detached and therefore gives the greatest opportunities to disregard the humanity of subjects, absolute rulers are most prone to abuse it. Consequently, absolute rule is to be avoided, as Fielding argues after showing us the gypsies' king.

And at the very center of all is the feeling heart, the semidivine instrument by which the lover is made aware of the special humanity of another human being; by which the ruler recognizes his obligations to the humanity of the ruled; by which all people are aware that they are dealing with others like themselves and not objects; by which, finally, communication is made possible. Through it, ones reaches out of the enclosure of the self. When the awareness of this reaching is registered within the self, internal harmony ensues.

IV

The Psychology of the Novels

IN THE PREFACE to *Joseph Andrews,* Fielding admits that he has introduced black vices despite his program of ridiculing only foibles. Since he is following real human nature, he says, he cannot omit vices: humanity cannot be faithfully imitated without reproducing the consequences of violent passions. For that matter, his practice suggests that the springs of action—or at least of plot in fiction—are violent passions, not foibles. Though rewards and punishments are registered within the mind, man must act in the world outside, where his preoccupations must inevitably conflict with those of others. Plot is a series of such conflicts. Though Cervantes is one of Fielding's models, Molière is his master in drama; conflict of passions, not the exhibition of one deluded consciousness, constitutes his imitation of the real world. Adams' absentmindedness would be insignificant without his argumentative dogmatism, which brings him to the verge of battle with various equally violent acquaintances. And there would be no novel at all without Lady Booby's lust and Joseph's passionate chastity.

Vanity, the master passion of the comic psychology which dominates the first novel and influences considerably the themes and structures of the other two, is basic in the moral statement of *Joseph Andrews.* Vanity, the source of all passional violence—"All our passions are thy slaves"—is the most confining of all passions for Fielding and the most widespread. No one is safe from some tincture of vanity; even Sophia and Amelia love to look in mirrors. The virtuous and experienced Wilson, in the course of narrating his own tale (his journey from indifference to a sense of another, his cousin Harriet who saves him socially and becomes the object of his morally saving love) says for Fielding that "vanity is the worst of passions, and more apt to contaminate the mind than any other . . . ." Selfishness, he says, is widespread, and "it is natural to hate and envy those who stand between us and the good we desire." In lust, ambition, even avarice, comparatively few persons stand between us and our desires, "but the vain man seeks pre-eminence; and everything which is excellent or praiseworthy in another renders him the mark of his antipathy" (III, iii). Even Parson Adams, the most unworldly of Fielding's creations, has his share of vanity, which is centered in the subjects of learning, the ministerial function, and the qualities of the school-master.[1]

In general, Fielding finds that vanity is a tractable vice. Wherever we are vain others can conveniently manipulate us. In small matters, vain people like Lady Booby or Slipslop or Pounce can be appeased by flattery. On a larger scale, vanity can lead to great acts of public usefulness, such as the establishment of colleges and hospitals. Joseph, in a lecture on charity, argues that the path to this virtue can be the vanity of the giver (III, vi), an argument which the author was to present in his own person in *Amelia:* "Nay, give me leave to wonder that pride, which is constantly struggling, and often imposing on itself, to gain some little pre-eminence, should so seldom hint to us the only certain as well as laudable way of setting ourselves above another man, and that is, by becoming his benefactor" (IV, iv).

Because passages of this sort clearly connect vanity and charity (following Mandeville, and perhaps Pope on the master passion), Mr. Battestin can plausibly argue that the thematic unity of the first novel lies in the balance achieved between a satiric thesis of vanity and a positive antithesis of charity. Such a view, I think, slightly blurs the focus of the book. In his preface Fielding says that vanity and hypocrisy are his subjects, and it is evident that everything in the novel is explicable by these qualities, not by their opposites. If we consider charity a theme equal to vanity, we cannot sufficiently excuse the absurdity of Adams; if vanity is predominant, then Adams becomes the perfect illustration of inevitable imperfection in even the best human character. In the first case, we must make central the narrative of Wilson, thereby giving structural primacy to an inactive stretch (which I grant that Fielding is using symbolically, as he uses the Man of the Hill's account in *Tom Jones*), an unlikely arrangement for a confirmed Aristotelian. In the other, the encounter with the vicious squire—the extreme in that self-enclosed vanity which poses the greatest threat to all the virtuous—is the central climax. If we abandon the issue of climax and argue instead for thematic iteration as the source of unity, then the story of Leonora the flirt is irrelevant to charity but directly concerned with vanity.[2] While charity is clearly the positive answer to the follies exposed, the actual exposure of those follies across the spectrum of human nature is, as Fielding said, the substance of the novel.

But vanity and its subordinate passions do not always work alone, nor is their operation uniform. The scene between Lady Booby and Mrs. Slipslop early in *Joseph Andrews* is constructed on the principle "that passions operate differently on the human mind, as diseases on the body, in proportion to the strength or weakness, soundness or rottenness, of the one and the other"; hence "the different operations of this passion of love in the gentle and cultivated mind of the Lady Booby, from those which it effected in the less polished and coarser disposition of Mrs. Slipslop" (I, vii). Despite the irony—the moral difference between the two "operations" is only that between psychological and physical rape—the distinction is meaningful. Environment—particularly social education—can help to repress the overt aggression of violent passions by transferring it from the realm of unthinking action (Mrs. Slipslop) to that of conscious imagination (Lady Booby). As in Pope's famous lines, social pressures can here act the part of reason. Furthermore, a favorite practice of Fielding as novelist, hinted at in *Tom Jones* when he speaks of the variety which he has created within the same social strata and occupations, is to combine the various atoms—passions, reflective ability, disposition, social position, education, habit, occupation—in different ways, to see what the resultant may be. In the Lady Booby-Joseph case, the power which society gives to aristocrats over footmen can support the passions in achieving their desires; later in the novel, the vicious squire can count on much of society's approval in his wish to rape Fanny. Indeed, society itself can abet certain kinds of passions, as Fielding ironically observes: he says that Lady Booby is sorely tempted by Joseph's beauty, and hopes that his women readers, when he describes his hero, will "bridle their rampant passion for chastity, and be at least as mild as their violent modesty and virtue will permit them" in judging her (I, viii). As a social satirist, Fielding is notable for his early insistence that comstockery can be as unsavory as the motives for excess.

The most extended study of passion in the novel is Lady Booby. Early and late, her mind is a battlefield, in which vanity always wins. Within this mind, the outgoing passions, Love, Honour, and Pity, are on Joseph's side; self-enclosed Pride and Revenge are against him, "and thus the poor lady was tortured with perplexity, opposite passions distracting and tearing her mind different ways" (I, ix). Her dismissal of Joseph is for therapeutic, not moral reasons; she thinks her mind will be more at rest with him away, and finds it convenient to think also that she is pushing aside temptation. When we meet her later, we find that she again is subjected to mental disturbances by a succession of various passions, which returned the day after she dismissed Joseph (IV, i). Evidently her disposition is itself made up of a confused conflict of passions.

Her imaginative wallowing in sensual pleasures does not permit direct, outward joys of the sort which Joseph and Fanny can have. Joseph, who has caused the fancies, has also put her pride in great public danger: such acts as attempting to send Fanny to a bridewell are beneath her as an aristocrat, and through them she has completely committed herself to the pursuit of a footman. There is no peace for her, as Fielding suggests in the title of Book IV, Chapter xiii, where her absurd similarity to a tragic heroine is alluded to: "The history, returning to the Lady Booby, gives some account of the terrible conflict in her breast between love and pride." And her single case is no more than a critical example of the mind affected by a mixture of passions. As generally in Fielding's psychology, where a variety of passions dominates a mind over a long period of time, their combination constitutes the character; in such a mind the disposition must be selfishly indrawn.

The relations between the basic disposition and the overlay of different passions allow for the permanence within variety which Fielding claims as his province in his comment on the universality of the Tow-wouses: "where extreme turbulency of temper, avarice, and an insensibility of human misery, with a degree of hypocrisy, have united in a female composition, Mrs. Tow-wouse was that woman; and where a good inclination, eclipsed by a poverty of spirit and understanding, hath glimmered forth in a man, that man hath been no other than her sneaking husband" (III, i). Disposition, as I have earlier noted, is something antecedent to the passions but deducible from them, "given," and not subject to destruction, though it may be modified and camouflaged by education. Mrs. Tow-wouse's passions, all connected with her presumably selfish disposition, seem to reinforce each other, though they must be kept within acceptable limits by her social and economic condition. Her husband, whose good disposition is constantly checked by a bad passion (cowardice) and who is unable to see the world clearly, is inevitably a butt of comic frustrations. While Fielding is centrally concerned to reveal vanity and hypocrisy in *Joseph Andrews,* he does not stop with these elements of character, but goes on to make a serious attempt to support the comic actions with "nature": a coherent system of psychology made up of passional building blocks.

In the introductory metaphor of *Tom Jones,* Fielding securely affirms his system of human qualities as fixed ingredients which he can mix together to form the compounds evident in real life: "we shall represent human nature at first to the keen appetite of our reader, in that more plain and simple manner in which it is found in the country, and shall hereafter hash and ragoo it with all the high French and Italian seasoning of affectation and vice which courts and cities afford" (I, i). Halfway through the novel, he repeats that he is specifically and consciously working with discrete elements. He warns his critics not to "find out too near a resemblance between certain characters here introduced; as, for instance, between the landlady who appears in the seventh book and her in the ninth . . . there are certain characteristics in which most individuals of every profession and occupation agree. To be able to preserve these characteristics, and at the same time to diversify their operations, is one talent of a good writer. Again, to mark the nice distinction between two persons actuated by the same vice or folly is another" (X, i). Though there are times when Fielding is interested in the spontaneous, unformulable psychological response (Richardson's subject), most of his characters as comic figures growing out of plot and theme are made up of clear and distinct mental elements.

The first women in the novel are fine examples of the combinations of simple passions disguised through concern for society's responses. In Mrs. Wilkins, the passion for prudery is as much a consequence of vanity as wilfulness had been for Lady Booby: "It will not be wondered at that a creature who had so strict a regard to decency in her own person should be shocked at the least deviation from it in another" (I, iii). When she goes to the village to discover the mother of the waif, "as it is the nature of a kite to devour little birds, so it is the nature of such persons as Mrs. Wilkins to insult and tyrannize over little people" in compensation for her servility to her superiors (I, vi). As always, the vice consists of denying the individual humanity of others for the sake of feeding one's own vanity. Bridget Allworthy is another of the same stamp, a copy, Fielding tells us, of the wintry prude in Hogarth's "Morning." Since she runs her life in accordance with the mechanical rules of society rather than through spontaneous feeling as refined by social breeding, she has the considerable problem of encouraging Captain Blifil with propriety, "for she was a strict observer of all rules of decorum" (I, xi). Her underlying lecherousness, covered by physical and moral appearances so like Mrs. Wilkins', helps to solidify the combination as true not only of an individual but of a kind. It becomes the definitive manifestation of a particular disposition.

In the attitude of Captain Blifil toward his brother, particularly after the brother has informed him of his politic warning to Allworthy, Fielding again shows the working of compound passions, in this case supporting rather than clashing with each other. The captain had always despised his brother as a weakling while envying his superior mind. Envy, says Fielding, is aggravated by contempt, "and very much afraid I am, that whenever an obligation is joined to these two, indignation and not gratitude will be the product of all three" (I, xiii). After his marriage, Captain Blifil, the most aggressive, cold, and selfish person in the novel before the appearance of Lady Bellaston, "began to treat the opinions of his wife with that haughtiness and insolence which none but those who deserve some contempt themselves can bestow, and those only who deserve no contempt can bear" (II, vii). The novel's showpiece of irony, the lonely death of the captain while he is absorbed in selfish thoughts, is a direct consequence of his complete and self-willed enclosure within himself.

The mind's subjection to discrete pressures at any given moment is memorably illustrated in George Seagrim's famous psychomachia when he is tempted by Tom's money. George had enough good nature to carry Tom's letter to Sophia, "for he bore as much gratitude toward him as he could, and was as honest as men who love money better than any other thing in the universe, generally are" (VI, xii). His mental conflict, an argument between Conscience and Avarice about the sixteen guineas which Sophia was sending Tom, was solved by Fear, which said that the difference between the earlier theft of five hundred pounds and this temptation was "safety; for that the secreting the £500 was a matter of very little hazard; whereas the detaining the sixteen guineas was liable to the utmost danger of discovery" (VI, xiii). George's situation, Fielding argues, is exemplary, not unique. Even the violent Westerns are unique only in that their passions are exhibited through direct speech and action; for those without the controls of conscience, reason, and prudence, all motivation is affected by single passions in conflict, the strongest winning dominance at the moment.

In the behavior and psychology of Sophia toward the middle of the novel, Fielding shows that even for his paragons placidity is impossible when external forces are complex and intractable. While she had cheerfully and courageously set out on the adventures which Richardson referred to as "inn-frequenting," when she became involved in ambiguous situations, she was subject to qualms and conflicts. Her recent activity had led to a condition almost as unsettling as that brought on by guilt, though not so painful or unhappy: she "had been lately so distracted between hope and fear, her duty and love to her father, her hatred to Blifil, her compassion, and . . . her love for Jones, . . . that her mind was in that confused state which may be truly said to make us ignorant of what we do, or whither we go, or rather, indeed, indifferent as to the consequence of either" (X, ix). At a later stage, a slight dishonesty causes her more actual discontent: after the scene in which she lies to Lady Bellaston about Tom's identity, she spends a sleepless night, "for the frame of her mind was too delicate to bear the thought of having been guilty of a falsehood, however qualified by circumstance" (XIII, xii).

Usually, Sophia's emotional condition is the resultant of a few morally neutral passions, a controlling superb disposition, and the outer situation. At least once, however, in describing her feelings when she left Upton, Fielding casts an unexpected and significant glance at the human psyche outside his system, at that unconscious which was Richardson's province. Sophia, he says, was afraid of being overtaken by her father, though not by Tom: "nay, to confess the truth, I believe she rather wished than feared it; though I might honestly enough have concealed this wish from the reader, as it was one of those secret spontaneous emotions of the soul to which the reason is often a stranger" (XI, iii). Her underlying disposition, or instinct, or inclination, is one of loving, outgoing good will; it is antecedent to the social, prudential, and legalistic reason, and even to the forces of religion. That this out-going good will is also, in this case, self-gratifying merely confirms Sophia's good fortune in having a naturally harmonious mind. Sophia's emotions are almost all attractive and perfectly natural to a virtuous girl in love, so that we are likely to find her passions leading to good rather than bad. Indeed, since she is always aware of the dictates of prudence, and except for "secret spontaneous emotions" makes no improper commitments, her passions are the effluences of love, and any manifestations of excitement are really the governable "animal spirits."

The emotions of other, less admirable figures are usually the source of unpleasantness, as witness the activities and natures of Blifil (who wants to marry Sophia to gratify both avarice and hatred), Lady Bellaston (the prey of pride and lust), and such unfortunate minor characters as the avaricious old Nightingale and the envious and malicious Northerton. Old Nightingale is permanently unhappy in his avarice, and Blifil more unhappy in his combination of vices. Unhappiest of all in any one situation, however, is Tom, for his psychological confusion as he sits in jail fearful that he has committed murder and incest is complicated by a very tender conscience (XVI, x). Blifil's mind, like those of Wild and Plato's tyrant, must be hell because of the violence of his passions and its fear of mankind's hatred; Tom's, because of his sensitivity to the awful distortion which his internal good will has suffered in its excursion into the world. Tom's condition is temporary and remediable, since his motivation—the direct expression of his disposition acting through the passions—has been good. Blifil's and Lady Bellaston's lives are continuous hells, regardless of the social outcome of specific actions.

Though violent passions, the sign of unusual selfishness, are always objectionable (if Fielding formally approves a passion against vice, he demonstrates no great liking for it, since even Allworthy may err under its influence), nonetheless an exuberant nature, signifying not passion but abundant energy reaching out of oneself, is admirable. Sophia, "with the highest degree of innocence and modesty, had a remarkable sprightliness in her temper" (IV, v). Tom was "a thoughtless, giddy youth, with little sobriety in his manners, and less in his countenance; and would often very impudently and indecently laugh at his companion for his serious behavior" (III, v). On the day Allworthy's recovery began, Fielding says that Tom easily showed the effects of drinking, because his "naturally violent animal spirits" were set off by his benefactor's improvement and augmented by wine. Like Northerton's later, Tom's disposition merely acts more extremely along its normal lines, "for drink, in reality, doth not reverse nature, or create passions in men which did not exist in them before. It takes away the guard of reason, and consequently forces us to produce those symptoms which many, when sober, have art enough to conceal" (V, ix). Another moralist of the time—Swift, or Johnson, for example—might proceed to argue for staying sober and keeping guard, but for Fielding the innate disposition, the underlying nature, not the guard, determines morality.

The consequences and the psychology of Tom's drunkenness are revealing. He sings Sophia's beauty and his total love for her; but having raised the idea of sexual love, he straightway sinks to the ground with the receptive Molly, a female animal stinking and sweating from manuring the fields. Lust, which is the animal part of love, has become dominant with the removal of the restraints of reason and conscience, though not of good nature. Tom's passion demands its gratification, but only with the good will of another. In his defense, Fielding observes that "he was not at this time perfect master of that wonderful power of reason which so well enables grave and wise men to subdue their unruly passions, and to decline any of these prohibited amusements" (V, x). Even when it has been brutalized, the passion of love is positive, and is therefore preferable to the negation of stoicism.

A youthful disposition toward sexual love is an ingredient (though an ambiguous one, as witness Molly) in the virtuous disposition toward love. "Young men of open, generous dispositions are naturally inclined to gallantry, which, if they have good understandings, as was in reality Tom's case, exerts itself in an obliging complacent behavior to all women in general" (IV, v). By contrast, though egged on to the match by avarice and ambition, and later by sadism, Blifil is not much interested in Sophia: "his appetites were by nature so moderate that he was able, by philosophy, or by study, or by some other method, easily to subdue them" (VI, iv). Unlike Richardson's or Jane Austen's characters, Fielding's heroes and heroines do not have a protective barrier of fear and sensitivity; and when two good dispositions meet, no time is wasted on the slow growth of love. Caution is not characteristic of the good disposition, which can greatly triumph in human relations or be swiftly defeated.

Acting on the socially acceptable passions does not guarantee peace, at least in the short run, since only in optimal situations do they agree with the more self-pleasing ones. Natural appetites, however inappropriate to the moment, cannot simply be nullified. When exiled, Tom is resolved, through honor, despair, and gratitude to Allworthy, not to drag Sophia to ruin; he is very pleased with himself, but immediately becomes miserable at the thought of leaving Sophia. To add to the difficulties of achieving serenity, certain impulses of vanity, the most powerful of the passions, may animate what seem to be wishes for virtue. Sophia was tempted to agree to her father's demands out of love for him and the religious desire to obey; and when she thought of herself as a martyr, "she felt an agreeable tickling in a certain little passion which, though it bears no immediate affinity either to religion or virtue, is often so kind as to lend great assistance in executing the purposes of both" (VII, ix). Even the most outgoing passions cannot express themselves purely when countervailing passions are present. Only in wedded love, in a setting of social and economic security away from such depravities as abound in London, can such purity be assured.

Though passions are the cause of all evil, they are also often the source of noble feelings and actions. In theory, Fielding considers them neutral, in the spirit of Aristotle's *Ethics* and Pope's *Essay on Man*. While he does not in practice show any passion but courage as neutral (love, whether a passion or a disposition, is always good in *Tom Jones*), he does try to give all the passions a measure of justice, particularly as they appear nakedly in Squire Western. Western, he says, "had not the least command over any of his passions; and that which had at any time the ascendant in his mind hurried him to the wildest excesses" (VI, vii). At most times before his daughter's choice arouses the blind vanity associated with his class and position, they lead him on engaging paths. For example, when he saw two men fighting with a third, he immediately jumped in, "and, with more gallantry than policy, espoused the cause of the weaker party" (V, xi). He spontaneously speaks up for Tom when Tom does not threaten his rule over Sophia; he delights in their coming felicity at the end; he yields to Sophia whenever his fundamental vanity does not interfere. He rather likes his sister, who is precisely his female counterpart.

Indeed, the passions of the older Westerns and their consequent susceptibility to management become a major source of plot in the novel, as well as of humor. The discovery of Sophia's love for Tom and the forced match with Blifil are directly precipitated by Mrs. Western's vanity, which leads her to believe herself privy to the motives of others. In response to Honour's insults, Mrs. Western goes off "with a countenance so full of rage that she resembled one of the furies rather than a human creature" (VII, viii), and Honour achieves her aim of being discharged. When Fielding has put his plot in danger by allowing Western to close in on his daughter before her arrival in London, he saves himself brilliantly with an appeal to "nature," to Western's class-determined passion for fox-hunting: "we are not to arraign the squire for any want of love for his daughter; for in reality he had a great deal; we are only to consider that he was a squire and a sportsman" (XII, ii). At a later stage in the haggling over how to dispose of Sophia in marriage, the passions of the brother and sister prevent disaster by canceling each other. Even Sophia, not a manipulator, finds that she can make her aunt support a competing candidate through appeals to her vanity, thereby dividing the threats.

Western is that favorite figure of eighteenth-century speculation, the natural man, unaffected either by social rules or by religion, and a mixed lot he is. Considerations of comic art aside, his significance in Fielding's ethical or psychological theory is purely that of an extreme example. His instincts are reasonably generous, but organized in no consistent pattern; he can be a major force for bad, as witness his brutal indifference to the misery of his wife and his mistreatment of Sophia when she opposes his will. He is an instrument of others, never an initiator, because he is led by his passions; and instruments are notoriously more often used by the evil than by the good. He is incapable of sustained happiness, since anything can put him into a violent passion; temporary peace is only achieved through sedatives, whether good (Sophia's playing) or bad (wine). Being totally unreasonable, he is incapable of contentment of the sort that Allworthy or Wilson or Booth can enjoy.[3] Both he and his sister are unable to see around them because of the distortions within: "as the brother never foresaw anything at a distance, but was most sagacious in immediately seeing everything the moment it happened, so the sister eternally foresaw at a distance, but was not so quick-sighted to objects before her eyes . . . and, indeed, both their several talents were excessive; for, as the sister often foresaw what never came to pass, so the brother often saw much more than was actually the truth" (X, viii). Two of Fielding's favorite targets, the booby squire and the court bluestocking, are thus fundamentally the same victims of the same vanity. Both are self-enclosed, Locke's helpless lunatics, unable to act effectively in a world they cannot see.

Despite these superb humors characters, *Tom Jones,* as all of Fielding's critical comments would suggest, is an Aristotelian book, with the concentration not so much on the individual peculiarities of psyche as on the over-all fable.[4] The important issue is not the psychological idiosyncrasy of Tom but Fielding's intellectual conception of the protected young foundling bursting with good nature who is turned adrift in a chaotic world. He is rewarded for his virtue at the end with the ideal combination for mental content: a country estate and the finest wife in the world. Outer sources of disturbance are eliminated, or rather, as Wilson had indicated in the first novel, the outer environment is merely that most conducive to content. Since Tom's disposition is excellent and he has no dominant passion, he can get out of himself into the harmony that is Sophia and the country, and from them in turn receive healthful, civilizing emanations. The harmony of the novel, a reflection of this Eden, is too full to allow for dominance by any one character or element.

While Fielding intended *Amelia* to be as much a study of psychological actuality as Richardson's successes, he fails at least in part because the apparatus which he brings to the examination of his characters is merely the detached, abstract system of psychology which had served other purposes in his comic novels. Applied seriously, in an analysis of real people living through time—not ideal or emblematic ones caught in a permanent moment—its assumption of either changelessness or arbitrary change leads only to sentimentality, not perceptiveness—the same reason, essentially, for the failure of Richardson's last novel.

In *Amelia* even more seriously and copiously than in its predecessors, guilt and other painful emotions provide considerable mental disturbance, needing nothing from outside to stimulate the misery. Booth, guilty of unfaithfulness and extravagance, is full of vague premonitions when he and Amelia return to their apartment to find that it has been searched: "fear is never more uneasy than when it doth not certainly know its object; for on such occasions the mind is ever employed in raising a thousand bugbears and phantoms, much more dreadful than any realities, and, like children, when they tell tales of hobgoblins, seems industrious in terrifying itself" (VI, iv). At a slightly later stage, Fielding compares the innocence, hope, and good reputation of Amelia in distress with the stormy mind, the loss of reputation and friends, and the basic hopelessness of Mrs. Ellison (VIII, iii); though the evocation of reputation and friends may be purely hortatory, Fielding surely accepts the mental conditions as fact. As with Tom in jail, the better and more serene the mind, the less habituated it is to storminess and the slighter the impropriety can be that leads to the storms; after James's incriminating challenge to Booth was sent to Amelia and she thought that her husband was further involved with Miss Matthews, she called him a scoundrel to her children, and in consequence passed a sleepless night, "her gentle mind torn and distracted with various and contending passions, distressed with doubts, and wandering in a kind of twilight which presented her only objects of different degrees of horror, and where black despair closed at a small distance the gloomy prospect" (XI, ix).

Also as in the earlier novels, the sexual passion is ambiguous, being available for the greatest good and the greatest evil. Here, however, the emphasis is on its dangers. Ambition is bad only in cruel and savage people, and avarice rarely appears except among the base; but love, resident in the noblest minds, can destroy their very nobility: "not only tenderness and good nature, but bravery, generosity, and every virtue are often made the instruments of effecting the most atrocious purposes of this all-subduing tyrant"

(VI, i). When it is manifestly disinterested, as are Booth's and Atkinson's love for Amelia, it ennobles the possessor, making him the object of the love of others. Miss Matthews developed her passion when she heard Booth talk of his wife, and Mrs. Bennet married the sergeant because his adoration of Amelia demonstrated a great capacity for love and therefore the possession of many other virtues. Both of these women, one slightly tainted and the other corrupt, are partly exploiting love, seeking to transfer to themselves the love aroused by another whose nature deserves it. They are therefore responding not out of a purely good disposition, but out of a wish to acquire the benefits of such a disposition.

Where Fielding's system is insufficient in the face of reality, as in the peculiar emotionality of some of his characters, he contents himself with noting that unexplainable passions exist. The hints of inconsistency in the other novels—as in Sophia's fleeting thought of the pleasure of martyrdom—become here almost the basis of a theory that character is undiscoverable (as Locke implied and Sterne proved). Miss Matthews, for example, is one moment gentle and the next bloodthirstily delighted at the thought of having murdered her seducer; Fielding simply says that this is the way some people, notably the English, behave, and cites the revolutionaries of 1745 and a cherubic wanton as evidence. Booth's own irresponsibility and weakness are not explained as the inevitable concomitants of a good disposition—as Tom's sexual promiscuity was thus derived—but are to be taken as given, elements which happen to coexist with such a disposition. There may be an increase of realism here, in that Booth is not so evidently cut to fit the conception of "fable" as his predecessors, but there is also a loss in significance and inevitability.

The trouble is not that we demand system, but that Fielding at times accepts and at other times repudiates system. Miss Matthews may be, like Lady Booby, primarily the distorted consequence of mixed and inconsistent passions. But she is not a burlesque figure like her early model. We are to take her as a serious threat; consequently, we insist that Fielding explain her more fully, and he cannot. Lady Booby will do as an anticipation of Strindberg's Miss Julia, because she is a gross exaggeration. But Miss Matthews cannot be the real Dido. Fielding detests the real thing too much for the sympathy essential to seriousness.

In Booth, Fielding creates a worldly theoretician on psychology, to be a foil for Dr. Harrison's Christian emphasis on free choice. Booth philosophizes about the fact that distance really does make people forget, and when Miss Matthews laughs he answers "that the doctrine of the passions had been always his favorite study; that he was convinced every man acted entirely from that passion which was uppermost" (III, iv). As an example, he cites Captain James's saving devotion to him when he was almost fatally wounded: "The behavior of this man alone is a sufficient proof of the truth of my doctrine, that all men act entirely from their passions; for Bob James can never be supposed to act from any motives of virtue or religion, since he constantly laughs at both; and yet his conduct toward me alone demonstrates a degree of goodness which perhaps few of the votaries of either virtue or religion can equal" (III, v). Booth's confusion about the nature of the coldest character in the novel is evidence of how a theory (very soothing to his sense of failure) can confine a man and hide the world from him as thoroughly as if he had Western's passions. Reason, like prudence, can be perverted and thereby contribute to self-enclosure.

In Booth's last conversation on the subject, he claims a new understanding of motivation. His religious doubts had arisen from the theory he had expounded, that man acts completely from his passions, which are themselves predetermined and beyond choice, so that his actions cannot be morally judged. To counter the argument, Dr. Harrison temporarily accepts the notion of action from passion, but concludes "that religion to be true which applies immediately to the strongest of these passions, hope and fear; choosing rather to rely on its rewards and punishments than on that native beauty of virtue which some of the ancient philosophers thought proper to recommend to their disciples" (XII, v). This seems something of an endorsement of Mrs. James's comment to her husband that Amelia's virtue "hath the best guard in the world, which is a most violent love for her husband" (XI, i). By implication, the only way to fight passion is with passion. As always with Fielding, religion is most valuable as a system of ethics justified by its psychological operation, as the perennially popular source of "peace of mind."

It is not clear, however, how a man is to get himself out of his intolerable situation; having a passion is evidently not an act of will, and Amelia's perfection is no less arbitrary than her sister's viciousness. Furthermore, the passion-dominated mind, as Fielding always insisted, is incapable of the reflection and the delays required to make religious hope and fear powerful. Colonel James's hope is to enjoy Amelia *now*, not paradise later. How are people like the noble lord, Colonel James, the lawyer Murphy, Amelia's sister Betty, and Mrs. Ellison to adjust themselves toward fear and hope in the distant future? Certainly, Fielding's unsentimental disposal of them does not support Harrison's answer. Presumably they, as well as the pimp Trent and his wife, Justice Thrasher, and the many others who are in some way ill disposed have had an improper education, but to accept this condition is in effect to adopt the view of the cynical politician who tells Harrison that justice is chimerical in "as corrupt a nation as ever existed under the sun" (XI, ii). Is it possible in this society to develop the seeds of virtue which most people are supposed to have?

If sentimentalism involves a persuasion that at bottom all men are good and are capable of becoming good given the right circumstances, then Fielding is not a sentimentalist. Booth's various comments on the selfish motivation of mankind—its tendencies to act toward the gratification of the passion that is uppermost, so that we are all to some extent Squire Westerns—are frequently supported in the person of the author. Yet *Amelia* is not formally pessimistic about human nature. To the heroine's complaints, Dr. Harrison says, "The nature of man is far from being in itself evil, it abounds with benevolence, charity, and pity, coveting praise and honor, and shunning shame and disgrace. Bad education, bad habits, and bad customs, debauch our nature, and drive it headlong as it were into vice" (IX, v). By implication, society is the cause of vice, a view that would explain the evil in which Mrs. Ellison participates as a bawd to her cousin. But it does not explain Colonel James's cold lustfulness or the colder lust of the lord himself; as some passages make clear, the flaws of both are constitutional. The arbitrariness of motivation and of destinies in *Amelia* suggests that eighteenth-century England is a crazy chaos of atomized people rather than a coherent and functioning society.

In most of his writings, however, Fielding does not accept the domination of character by arbitrary passion. Civilization does exist, as it could not in Booth's system. Reason is an element of the mind, and in its conflicts with the passions it often prevails, though sometimes at considerable cost. In the first two novels at least, the possible victory of a tolerant reason, which can adjust the violence of internal passion to the incoherence of external society, is generally shown in the disposal of the characters and the resolutions of the plots. The story and their constitutions allow Joseph and Wilson to live as gentlemen should, while the lovable but childish Adams is properly protected. Tom, by learning the danger of exuberance, by his achievement of Sophia, and by his smooth incorporation into the social stability and serenity of the Somerset squirearchy, is safely raised above any irregular call of the passions. Only in *Amelia* must a miraculous conversion revive the hero; only there is it implied that even a good man cannot overcome the assaults of temptation; and yet the heroine is evidence that such triumph is possible, given only the right psychological combination.

Though the basic disposition of the good man is benevolent—a corollary of his necessary religious feelings—nonetheless the right use of reason teaches him to protect himself and society against evil where he sees it. Thus Allworthy insists that Blifil does not deserve the kindness which the equally well-disposed though less reasonable Tom urges: "yet do not flatter him with any hopes of my forgiveness; for I shall never forgive villainy farther than my religion obliges me, and that extends not either to our bounty or our conversation" (XVIII, xi). He also condemns Tom's readiness to forgive Black George's dishonesty and ingratitude: "Such mistaken mercy is not only weakness, but borders on injustice, and is very pernicious to society, as it encourages vice" (XVIII, xi). As all his social pamphlets show, both from his analytical observation of life and by training as lawyer and magistrate, Fielding refused to fall into the trap of easy and universal benevolism; he insisted that evil was a reality and not an illusion, and that it had to be dealt with severely. Only the exercise of reason—which involves the assessment of how life develops in society—can guide the responsible judge.

Nevertheless, stoicism, which superficially seems to counsel what Fielding's plots imply—the rule of the emotions by the reason— he usually finds delusive.[5] It does not shape the emotions but rather suppresses them, with the result that the rare stoic who can practice his philosophy is as self-enclosed against feeling, against participation in the lives of others, as the completely passion-ridden. Such a man denies the importance of going outside the self, and in effect repudiates life. In *Tom Jones* Fielding expresses his contempt for thinkers like Square, who claim to know how to subdue desire and scorn pain and pleasure, "and this knowledge affords much delightful contemplation, and is easily acquired; but the practice would be vexatious and troublesome; and, therefore, the same wisdom which teaches them to know this teaches them to avoid carrying it into execution" (V, v). By contrast, Allworthy's mind "was, indeed, tempered with that philosophy which becomes a man and a Christian. He affected no absolute superiority to all pleasure and pain, to all joy and grief; but was not at the same time to be discomposed and ruffled by every accidental blast, by every smile or frown of fortune" (VI, iii). What the stoics counsel is against human nature and therefore impossible, a view which Fielding underscores in the Square-Molly sequence. Such a man as Square is vain in thinking himself above human calls, and hypocritical in disguising their expression.

Reason, which the stoics deify, is a guard which can hide what is bad as well as protect what is good. Acting as opportunistic prudence, an ability to calculate the odds for and against oneself, it may support the most despicable qualities of hypocrisy and manipulation. In all the Blifils, for example, Fielding gives us natures in which reason is an aggressive tool to be used to prey on the gullibility of society. Again, when it seems completely dispassionate, reason may simply be the tool of passionate self-enclosure, as with Colonel James. In his novels as in his other writings, Fielding equates the glorification of reason and the stoic contempt for the passions with a withdrawal from the world, and condemns them partly because they are so unnatural as to foster hypocrisy and partly because they constitute sterile self-enclosure. Pleasure is an inevitable concomitant of good action; despising pleasure is in effect denying one's humanity.

In addition to reason, the other factor that shapes the passions toward right action is religion. Reason is a restraining power which keeps vicious passions under control; but when it is the sole guide, it destroys the wish to act outside the self. Christianity, by contrast, is a motivating power, causing its subject to act in a charitable and well-disposed way, leading him out of himself to love others and work selflessly for them. The religious impulse is usually personal and absolute, whereas reason is predominantly social and relative. The disposition is largely affected by or allied with the private force of religion, while the relations of the passions and society are mediated through reason. The two animate, modify, and enforce each other in a serene mind. The formal Christian system is the perfect union of the two in society.

A good many times Fielding indicates how the demands of religion—nebulously, like reason, intermediate between a disposition and a passional appetite—conflict with the largely selfish passions; and sometimes the religious system, like any system, is not applicable to actual society. At least in *Joseph Andrews* and *Tom Jones*, though Fielding advocates religion he delights in showing that even the finest man will forget that earthly joy is vanity when he loves a beautiful woman. Sometimes the conflict is impossible to solve, just as in practice reason's advice to examine the objects of passion before acting may be impossible to follow.

In *Joseph Andrews*, when religion is in conflict with powerful social or emotive values, Fielding never opposes the religious truth though he sometimes emphasizes its irrelevance in the responses of ordinary people. In the argument between Trulliber and Adams, Mrs. Trulliber "begged him not to fight, but show himself a true Christian, and take the law of him" (II, xiv). After Fanny has been abducted, Adams lectures Joseph on his duty, as a Christian, to accept the blows of life with thanks; Joseph says he knows it is his duty, but he is nonetheless heartbroken. In both cases short-sighted individual passions have repelled the universal rules of religion; but in the first the motive is vanity, while in the second it is primarily love, the good disposition, a deep concern for the well-being of another. By implication, where the good disposition seems to come into conflict with the religious system, it is at least supportable, since it is fundamentally in accord with the spirit which underlies the system. Indeed, Fielding uses Adams himself to illustrate the human impossibility of following formal religious rules literally in practice: as Joseph points out, Adams' sermon on moderation, on not doting on others passionately, is immediately disproved by his own responses to the news of his son's drowning and his safety. While there is no question that in *Joseph Andrews* Fielding, as Mr. Battestin says, endorses the liberal church views of Barrow and Clarke, his ridicule of otherworldliness as an alternative to the warm facts of human feeling suggests a preference for the good disposition and its passions to systematic religion. No better system exists, but any system is intellectual and therefore no more than a form for feeling, which is primary.

By *Tom Jones,* the bumptious joy in life has been tempered to a more orthodox doctrine, and here all those in conflict with Christianity are satirized or lectured. Square, the deist, is a repellent hypocrite, though he is more worthy than the theologian Thwackum; enclosed within the dogmas of a sectarian faith, Thwackum repudiates the charity central to Fielding's Christianity. Western, without the slightest tincture of religion, is in consequence unreliable emotionally and morally. Even when the virtuous are specifically in conflict over the contrasting calls of passion and religion, religion is clearly right: though Tom and the lieutenant agree that a gentleman must fight when mistreated by another (his status in society, and therefore his vanity, would otherwise be wounded), Tom at least sees that religion legitimately forbids such killing. In contrast, Allworthy, who makes a variety of damaging errors, nonetheless is admirable because he always acts in accordance with fallible reason and is always ready to show the religiously charitable response to others; and Tom, who has the unconscious religion of good nature, is ready to accept conscious orthodoxy. By implication again, good nature is an antecedent and necessary ground for the growth of true religion. Good nature is vague and diffuse; religion directs it to its proper object, as reason protects it from misuse by the world.

In the last novel, religion is didactically affirmed (as in the discussion on dueling in *Tom Jones*), with Dr. Harrison presented as an ideal of both prudence and religion, not an eccentric like Adams. All the good people either are pious, like Amelia, or become so, like her husband. Fielding does introduce a young clergyman who reveres the form without feeling the essence of religion, but his role is confined to making this one point. Unwilling to allow the sort of ambiguity inherent in sinful samaritans (the thieving postilion and whorish chambermaid who preserve Joseph Andrews) and immoral pietists (the Blifils, Trulliber), Fielding here minimizes the inconsistency between religious profession and action. Providence is a frequent subject, and two major figures, Harrison and Amelia, are emphatically Christians in both speech and action. However, though Fielding attributes a great change in Booth to his reading of Barrow, he does not show its effects in his character or actions. The plot has nothing much to do with religion, the eventual felicity depending only on Harrison's persuading Booth and Amelia to come back to the country with him and on the discovery that a will has been forged. Without one of these conditions, nothing could have kept Booth from indefinite misery.

In the novels, Fielding has the problem of showing in apparently natural figures the eclectic psychological system which can be synthesized from his other writings, since he is serving up nature, making all the actions, if not probable, at least possible. The system remains pretty much the same throughout. Most men are born with both good and bad seeds, and the environment will presumably strengthen one or the other. Some men have no goodness, some no badness, with Blifil and Tom the closest approximations to the extremes among the major young figures.

In all character, disposition (presumably the relative proportion of the good and bad seeds) is at the core of the self. It is variously a mysterious separate essence which directs the other elements of the mind, or it is the resultant of the relations of these elements to each other. Of these, reason and religion (and perhaps conscience, which partakes of both) seem to stand between the disposition and the passions, though the relative position of the mental elements is ambiguous. Religion sometimes seems to be a basic element of the good disposition and sometimes a mechanism through which the disposition guides the passions. Reason is concerned with the direction and protection of the passions within society. Where the disposition is indrawn, reason becomes narrowly prudential and manipulative; where the self is well disposed, reason protects it against the manipulations of others.

In keeping with the shifting conditions within, the major passions, Vanity and Love, may alternatively be considered dispositions: they may be names for specific responses ("appetites") to real or imagined objects, in which case they are passions, or they may collectively describe the disposition of the mind inward or outward.

The interplay of these elements constitutes Fielding's psychological system. In the novels, growing uncertainty of its universal applicability accompanies an increased attempt to modify it to match reality. In *Joseph Andrews,* a professed exhibition of the ridiculous, character is explainable by a disposition toward vanity or toward charity, since qualities are simplified and exaggerated.

The minds of bad people are incoherent collections of passions at war with each other, with reason, and, where there is no social counterpoise (as with the roasting squire, who is under no authority), with society. Even good people have some elements of vanity—otherwise they would be divine—but these are so mild and so easily overcome by charity that they are amusing, not vicious. As our social scientists might put it, with all other factors held constant, the operations of the elements of vanity and charity are examined almost in isolation.

In *Tom Jones* Fielding's world has become both darker and more complex psychologically. The good and bad dispositions, and their correlatives love and vanity, are still dominant, but additional factors enter and previously subdued questions are made prominent. No one cares why Lady Booby and the roasting squire were so viciously subject to the extremes of selfishness, since Fielding had undertaken merely to show us phenomena, not to explain them. But by raising his hero and villain as half brothers, he directly faces us with the issue of determinism, of innate disposition, which can only partially be explained by contrasting paternities.[6] The good disposition, which in the earlier novel had been endangered only by ogres and physical force, here must face the possibilities of its own corruption because of the operation of faculties natural to it within a morally dangerous world. Betty, the chambermaid in *Joseph Andrews,* is a joke, if a slightly pathetic one; Tom Jones, the unintentional gigolo, who is forced to run one human being through the body and manipulate another (Lady Bellaston), is on the verge of being very serious indeed. No good person in *Joseph Andrews* needed to choose the lesser of two moral dangers to protect his disposition, as Tom must in sending a marriage proposal to Lady Bellaston. However, through the comic devices and rhetorical techniques which have been so widely investigated recently,[7] Fielding is able to apply his moral psychology effectively to the more complex reality of *Tom Jones.*

In *Amelia* Fielding's system seems less adequate in the face of complicated and determined reality. The heroine remains an example of the serene mind, emitting virtue and recording happy responses. But the hero, equally well disposed at bottom, reveals both a stubbornness of intellect and a deficiency of character which are disquieting inmates in a good mind. Tom Jones was heedless, but Booth is irresponsible; Tom professed himself a

Christian despite appearances to the contrary, but Booth believed man was so determined by his passions that he could make no moral choices. Evil characters are unmotivated and inconsistent at times; we do not see clearly how certain qualities fit together, and when Fielding describes Mrs. Ellison (VII, viii) and Mrs. James (VIII, ix) as good-natured, he seems to be abandoning the term, and perhaps the concept, in favor of exclusive reliance on religion. In *Amelia,* he seems overwhelmed by the perplexing, dominant superficiality of society, an external chaos which has forced a chaos upon the individual self. Where men without guidance are lost, exhortation, not exhibition or explanation, is his purpose.

V

Environment

FOR FIELDING, as I have argued throughout this essay, the center of existence is the self, and society is its sphere: the mind is the seat of happiness or misery, the world outside serving as material to furnish either. Staying within the self is painful evil, while virtuous joy derives from and supports that temperament which roves out into surrounding humanity and brings back the satisfaction of having felt and acted for others. Society has been formed as an arena for the good disposition, a medium through which it can fulfill itself.

With the dominant thinkers of his time, Fielding believed that to allow the individual the freest chance for moral action and therefore for happiness, society must provide him with an artificial social position to prevent the chaos of competition. The distinctions made by society must be maintained; and since they are outside the self, their proper maintenance will not interfere with the self's legitimate search for happiness. A hackney coachman will not be resentful because he is irrevocably the social inferior of a duke, for his happiness is internal. If both were not fixed in their positions, they would expect to engage in all the selfishness and self-torment of competing for superiority in a system which has few high places and many low ones. While the scope for good action by the coachman is smaller, it nonetheless exists. The happiness and virtue of both depend purely on the quality of interaction between their minds and the outside world; only the forms of interaction differ. And if they keep within their spheres in society, at the same time sympathizing with each other and with everyone else, they can be happy.[1] The social order is thus good in principle, though in practice it has been warped by individual and group selfishness.

Fielding is a reformer, wishing to remove the corruptions, not a revolutionary. Of these corruptions, the chief is the tendency by many, notably those born into high stations, to assume that the distinctions among people are moral rather than social; to forget that all men are equal before God and their consciences; to think, like Wild and other vicious great men, that the weaker orders are chattels of a different sort from themselves, not people whose passions, desires, and situations demand their sympathy.

Twice in his miscellaneous writings Fielding attempted to develop his social theories systematically. The early "Essay on Conversation" opens with the assertion that man is "an animal formed for, and delighted in, society" (*Works,* XIV, 245). Distinctions among people, and rules for observing them, are purely arbitrary: "all mere ceremonies exist in form only, and have in them no substance at all; but, being imposed by the laws of custom, become essential to good breeding . . . these ceremonies . . . constitute the only external difference between man and man" (*Works,* XIV, 252). Propriety consists in duly exercising the rights and fulfilling the obligations of one's own social position, whatever it may be. Decent social existence can obtain only if it is understood that "Men are superior to each other in this our country by title, by birth, by rank in profession, and by age; very little, if any, being to be allowed to fortune, though so much is generally exacted by it and commonly paid to it" (*Works,* XIV, 253). Fielding's alignment with an aristocratic scheme of society is nowhere more obvious than in this passage.[2] The usurpation of respect and privilege by the wealthy, a distortion of the basic structure of society as it has been built up over centuries, is as disturbing to the mind seeking a comprehensible world to act in as is the nobility's loss of sympathy with general humanity.

Toward the end of his career, Fielding attempted his most thorough examination of the social system outside the novels, in his pamphlet on the *Increase of Robbers.* While he carries the implications of his views on both principle and practice further than in the past, the views themselves are generally consistent with his other writings. He begins by asserting the classical conception of the state as a unified organism: just as the soul derives from the harmony of the parts of the body, and "as harmony doth from the proper composition of the several parts in a well-tuned musical instrument: In the same manner, from the disposition of the several parts in a state, arises that which we call the Constitution" (*Works,* XIII, 10). If the customs and conditions change, then the constitution inevitably changes, though its outward forms look the same. The "several parts" are, traditionally, nobility, gentry, and commoners.

Temporarily bypassing the first two orders, Fielding traces the changes in position of the common people from the medieval period and finds that they have become vastly more independent of the other two orders for a variety of reasons, the most important of which was "the introduction of trade. This hath indeed given a new face to the whole nation, hath in a great measure subverted the former state of affairs, and hath almost totally changed the manners, customs, and habits of the people, more especially of the lower sort. The narrowness of their fortune is changed into wealth; the simplicity of their manners into craft; their frugality into luxury; their humility into pride, and their subjection into equality" (*Works,* XIII, 14). Though the philosopher and the poet may complain about this change as moral decay, the politician "finds many emoluments to compensate all the moral evils introduced by trade," such as the nation's greatness and power and the advances in practical learning and comfort (*Works,* XIII, 14). At this point, Fielding seems to accept without criticism Mandeville's judgment of a commercial society. One evil consequence is that the power of money has increased disproportionately, so that it is beyond control by the old machinery. Except for an occasional tyrant in the country, the magistrate is helpless against this new wealth: "every riotous independent butcher or baker, with two or three thousand pounds in his pocket, laughs at his power, and every pettifogger makes him tremble" (*Works,* XIII, 16).

The social order has been disrupted by the downward seepage of luxury. Nobles try to live like princes and gentlemen like nobles, and "the tradesman steps from behind his counter into the vacant place of the gentleman. Nor doth the confusion end here; it reaches the very dregs of the people, who aspiring still to a degree beyond that which belongs to them, and not being able by the fruits of honest labour to support the state which they affect," give up jobs to become robbers, beggars, thieves (*Works,* XIII, 21-22). If luxury were kept to the great, their sense of honor might be some protection to society; and it is difficult to steal enough in ordinary ways to regain a great estate. But when luxury flows to tradesmen or laborers, it leads to robbery, since they may otherwise be forced into debts they cannot pay, the greatest shame for the commercially oriented.

Fielding's cure for vices, as earlier for the griefs of affliction, was removal of temptation, whether for individuals or for social orders. Of "the two great motives to luxury, in the minds of men," vanity is minor among the lower classes: they have as much vanity as their betters, but so little likelihood of gratifying it through conspicuous consumption that they sublimate by seeking the reputation of wealth, not its exhibition. Therefore, they are led to luxury by the other motive, love of pleasure; therefore, Fielding wants restrictions on public amusements and holidays, which provide their pleasures. Let "people of fashion and fortune" have their public follies, but legislate to prevent the "useful part of mankind" from being destroyed by theirs. So far as society is concerned, the lower people are to work, to suffer, and to be protected by the upper. The upper have responsibilities to the lower, which the best have signally fulfilled.[3] But when, as in contemporary England, they are largely corrupt and given over to trivia, little can be done except to show them their folly and to hope for better days. In his general theory of society, which is in the conservative pattern that goes back to Plato, Fielding sees no need for change; but he sees great deficiencies in practice because of widespread selfishness.

Fielding is also specific in his attachments of praise or blame to the various orders. Most of his comments on the upper classes, as might be expected from a comic writer, deal with their glaring shortcomings as models and guides. In a poem addressed to a virtuous nobleman, he indicates a major source of these failures: no matter how well-disposed, the nobility are insulated, self-enclosed against awareness of the miseries of others. He says, in "Of Good-Nature. To his grace the Duke of Richmond," that

> High on life's summit raised, you little know
> The ills which blacken all the vales below. . . .
> (*Works*, XII, 259)

But in most cases selfishness rather than good will accompanies such ignorance and determines the nobility in its antisocial behavior. In a corrupted society, the preface to the *Miscellanies* complains, the same crimes that bring the poor to Newgate lead the rich to respect and power.[4]

That the rich and noble are beyond the reach of laws and moralists Fielding sadly accepts; but he does several times hope that their vices and follies may be confined to themselves without corrupting others. In *The Champion* of February 19, 1740, for example, he says that if the rich will not limit their own luxuries, the next best thing would be for them to stop luring poorer people to expenses beyond their means (*Works*, XV, 208). In the *Charge to the Grand Jury* (1749) he agrees that the jury will not be able to do much against upper-class gamblers, but argues that if it punished the lower ones, perhaps the others could be shamed into reforming: "And to say the truth, to prevent gaming among the lower sort of people, is principally the business of society; and for this plain reason, because they are the most useful members of the society; which, by such means, will lose the benefit of their labour. As for the rich and great, the consequence is generally no other than the exchange of property from the hands of a fool into those of a sharper, who is, perhaps, the more worthy of the two to enjoy it" (*Works*, XIII, 215).

Only in the beginning of Fielding's career does the trading bourgeoisie fare better; later, he generally finds its members sacrificing their duty to society for the sake of pride and avarice. In the early poem "Of True Greatness" he attacks critics and academicians who think themselves great because they have conquered books and authors; this is self-enclosed pride and uselessness compared to the tradesman's courageous adventuring for the public good:

> Awake, ye useless drones, and scorn to thrive
> On the sweets gather'd by the lab'ring hive.
> Behold the merchant gives to thousands food,
> His loss his own, his gain the public good.
> Her various bounties Nature still confines,
> Here gilds her sands, there silvers o'er her mines:
> The merchant's bounty Nature hath outdone,
> He gives to all, what she confines to one.
> (*Works*, XII, 253)

But merchants who subordinate their country to their gains belong "with the meanest throng." A few years later, in the "Vernoniad" (1741), he also praises merchants for their independence and for the prosperity which they spread (*Works*, XV, 45, n. 31).

Elsewhere, Fielding suggests that a good many merchants jostle in the throng. In *Pasquin* the mayor and his aldermen, all tradesmen, keep busy selling the votes of the town to the highest bidder, while his wife and daughter are eager to provide anything at all to the nobility. *The Historical Register for the Year 1736* sets forth very clearly, in a speech by one trading patriot to three others, the besetting mercantile sin: "Lookye, gentlemen, my shop is my country. I always measure the prosperity of the latter by that of the former. My country is either richer or poorer, in my opinion, as my trade rises or falls; therefore, sir, I cannot agree with you that a war would be disserviceable: on the contrary, I think it the only way to make my country flourish; for as I am a swordcutter, it would make my shop flourish, so here's to war" (*Works*, XI, 266). What is good for General Motors, as an American official has neatly put it, is good for the country.

The Covent-Garden Journal, toward the close of Fielding's life, includes a bitter medieval attack on the self-enclosed pride of the wealthy in an analysis of society (*CGJ*, I, 294) and an essay which ironically recommends abolition of money, mainly to eliminate the distinctions between rich and poor (*CGJ*, I, 336-40). While these do not specifically refer to merchants, the omission of reference to rank seems to imply that the bourgeoisie is the target. In the *Journal*, Fielding's last work, he is fiercely angry with the fish merchants of London, again because they have put profit ahead of social duty. Fish are immensely plentiful, he says, yet the London fishmongers have conspired to keep prices so high that the poor—for whom nature seems to have destined this food—can never eat them (*Journal*, pp. 107-109). In these passages, Fielding is attacking not the class system but the selfish monopolizing of its rewards by merchants who have no concern for its welfare. Trade, which he sees as performing an essential and traditional part in the social system, has become a device for the destructive, unbalancing thrust of selfishness.

As a class the lower orders are no more attractive in Fielding's incidental writings than their superiors, since they have even cruder private passions to satisfy at the expense of their social duty; and as the novels more clearly indicate, force of circumstance, which is relatively minor as a corrupting influence on the others, works most powerfully on them. In *The Grub Street Opera* the servants of the Welsh squire who represents Walpole are completely concerted in their goals: "Fie upon't, William, what have we to do with master's losses? He is rich, and can afford it.—Don't let us quarrel among ourselves—let us stand by one another—for, let me tell you, if matters were to be too nicely examined into, I am afraid it would go hard with us all.— Wise servants always stick close to one another, like plums in a pudding that's overwetted, says Susan the cook" (*Works*, IX, 243). Fielding's views of servants in the major novels are further prefigured in his first extended fictional attempt, *Shamela*. When Booby gave Mrs. Jervis notice, she "made him a saucy answer— which any servant of spirit, you know, would, tho' it should be one's ruin" (*JA&S*, p. 314). He plans to send Shamela to his other house without her knowledge, but she discovers his intentions: "This is a piece of news communicated to us by Robin Coachman, who is entrusted by his master to carry on this affair privately for him: but we hang together, I believe, as well as any family of servants in the nation" (*JA&S*, pp. 314-15).

The selfish savagery of the lower orders—which Fielding derives from their necessarily repressive environment—is really the subject of the *Increase of Robbers*. There, he argues that a crying sin against social unity is the tendency of laborers to want high wages, despite the excellent but unenforced laws to limit them. He develops at length the argument, to be presented again in his posthumously printed *Journal*, that restricting wages by law and thus maintaining due proportion among the orders is beneficial to society (*Works*, XIII, 67ff). As always with Fielding (and with Goldsmith after him, as well as with most political commentators of the period), the standpoint is that of the middle gentry, who find themselves squeezed by the nobility and the very rich tradesmen from above, the tradesmen rising alongside, and the huge and dangerous mobs below.

In Fielding's *Proposal for . . . Provision for the Poor,* an appeal to the upper classes to sympathize with the conditions of the lower, he offers a drastically practical way to improve them and help society. He plans to erect workhouses, each to be a compound including a penal building for criminals, in most of which paupers would be clothed and fed in return for a reasonable amount of work and submission to supervision (an urban, ascetic

CCC). He insists that nothing can be done if the poor are idealized. Though his plan prevents them from wandering across county lines (to avoid vagrancy and its associated crimes), he sees no contravention of civil liberties or rights:

I should scarce apprehend, though I am told I may, that some persons should represent the restraint here laid on the lower people as derogatory from their liberty. Such notions are indeed of the enthusiastical kind, and are inconsistent with all order and all government. They are the natural parents of that licentiousness which it is one main intent of this whole plan to cure—which is necessarily productive of most of the evils of which the public complains; of that licentiousness, in a word, which among the many mischiefs introduced by it into every society where it prevails, is sure at last to end in the destruction of liberty itself. (*Works,* XIII, 181)

Where a stable order is assumed to be the main reason for the existence of society, and where man is to be judged by his moral condition and his usefulness to society, freedom of movement is mere frivolity. By the consequent destruction of liberty, Fielding means the inevitable movement of the commonwealth through democracy to tyranny, as Plato had sketched the process.[5] Like Milton he wants the distinction between liberty and license preserved.

The poor are unruly and would quickly destroy all order if allowed more freedom than is compatible with their function in society. However, this does not mean that they are the one guilty segment which must be repressed while the others may do what they wish. The proper society, to repeat, requires for its functioning that mankind be divided into fairly distinct classes, each with its due privileges and limitations. In this way, the economic system can be conveniently organized, and social coherence can be attained without competition for the same few prizes. People not only should be but are differently trained and educated for their positions. In the process the seeds of certain moral qualities are fostered or depressed: generosity, adventurousness, and humble industry, for example, may be characteristically developed virtues in descending social order, and disdain, avarice, and cruelty the equivalent vices.

The complex workings and relations of this social structure are the evident contents of Fielding's novels, which are aptly called the first great English novels of manners. Their very im-

petus is originally what Fielding saw as both formal and moral distortions of society in the most notable literary success of 1740.
Joseph Andrews and *Shamela* are both at least in part responses
to Richardson's *Pamela,* a subversive romance which encouraged
young gentlemen to conspire with wanton chambermaids to destroy all social order.

Joseph Andrews, therefore, has as its opening joke a reversal,
in which an aristocratic lecher, female, wishes to use a virtuous
young servant, male, for her pleasure, overlooking his possible
existence as a human being. Before her awareness of his sexual
attractiveness, she likes him as much as she does her pair of gray
mares (I, iii); after, she sees him only as a possible source of pleasure for herself. But Joseph, for reasons associated with a morality
which is antecedent to society, will not be a conspirator to breach
the social order. By implication Joseph's morality—based on what
he and Adams see as a Christian acceptance of one's condition—
is completely consistent with the formal arrangement of English
society, and he therefore resists the attempts of some in that society to exploit their positions improperly. Indeed, the response
of others to Joseph's position becomes a criterion of their moral
and social acceptability. If they are above him, then any tendencies to exploit him are improperly selfish and destructive of order.
If in the same class—as with the Tow-wouses—superciliousness or
coldness becomes evidence of the subversion of humanity by
money. Similarly, unusual kindness, like that of the poor postilion
or of Betty the chambermaid, suggests that human contact within
classes is easier than across them and that theft or sexual promiscuity may be largely caused by environment and does not necessarily
show a bad nature.

When the proper social distinctions are confounded, either
circumstances are unclear or selfishness has subverted the goal of
order. Wilson, whose responses are reliably civilized, is startled
to see a clergyman and a footman as close companions, and par-
donably thinks they may be thieves. Mrs. Slipslop, exploitively
interested in Joseph's welfare, begins a quarrel about precedence
with Miss Grave-airs, a prude who inhumanly refuses to ride in a
coach with the lame footman. When Mrs. Slipslop thinks her a
poor country gentlewoman, she is highly contemptuous, though
theoretically as a servant she should respect her social superior;
but when she discovers her to be the daughter of the rich steward

at a great estate—far lower socially than any gentlewoman—she regrets the quarrel, since the father would be most influential in the great houses of the area. Admirable social distinctions are here, as in all the novels, being broken for the sake of a selfish concern for the workings of money. Richardson and Fielding thus have opposite opinions of the contemporary social flux— Richardson eager to have the aristocracy conform to bourgeois standards while retaining its rank and distinction, and Fielding offended at the application of such standards. For Fielding, society had become so contaminated by the self-enclosed pride of the powerful—whether in the brutal whimsicality of the upper classes or in the businessman's cold money worship—that the middle gentry and the virtuous and useful lower classes were being harried out of existence. They could not beat the exploiters, and should not join them.

But businessmen, in Fielding's genteel world, can be socially avoided. Their hypocrisies may cause political difficulties, but need not directly affect the weak so greatly as the vices of country tyrants. When Wilson's universally dishonest competitors forced him out of the wine trade, he was able to retire to the country and live the good life of the middle gentry. Even Peter Pounce, Fielding's most elaborate study of a capitalist, is after all a steward in a great lady's household, no more modern than Chaucer's Reeve. Fielding deplored the effects of money, but he could see them only as indications of corruption, not as part of a major change leading to another moderately stable system of society.

While Wilson and his visitors are talking, Fielding gives us an example of a more immediate and permanent divisive element in society: the son of the local squire rides by and, for his amusement, kills the dog of Wilson's daughter. Another squire, a lunatic devil who illustrates the effects of contempt for humanity combined with locally unlimited power, first sets his hunting dogs on Joseph, Fanny, and Adams, and then subjects them to greater discomforts and perils. The only answers to him and to his grander equivalent Lady Booby (both of whom can subvert secular law) are wealth or individual integrity associated with rural gentility (Wilson, if he were richer; Allworthy, in the next novel) or with the church (Adams). While the much later *Increase of Robbers* shows that in the intervening years Fielding learned a great deal more about what was happening to society, he never abandoned the ideal of the first novel. Perhaps that is why his tone becomes less and less joyous as he proceeds.

In *Tom Jones* Fielding formally sets out to cover the variety of manners in England. There are consequently all sorts of acute comments on both the qualities suitable for the various stations in life and the qualities which they actually displayed. In contrast to such novelists as Richardson (whose mistakes in current manners Fielding joyfully points out at all opportunities), he insists that the man who does not have wide experience in his society is disqualified from writing about it. As in *Joseph Andrews*, his focus is on observation and exhibition, not on a theoretical examination of change. The novelist must have "conversation," knowledge of life through living it; furthermore, it "must be universal, that is, with all ranks and degrees of men; for the knowledge of what is called high life will not instruct him in low; nor, *è converso,* will his being acquainted with the inferior part of mankind teach him the manners of the superior. And though it may be thought that the knowledge of either may sufficiently enable him to describe at least that in which he hath been conversant, yet he will even here fall greatly short of perfection; for the follies of either rank do in reality illustrate each other." The novelist's own manners will improve if he knows low and high, "for in the one he will easily find examples of plainness, honesty, and sincerity; in the other of refinement, elegance, and a liberality of spirit; which last quality I myself have scarce ever seen in men of low birth and education" (IX, i). In this discussion, manners tend to shade into morals, as Lionel Trilling has acutely said of the novel generally. In the process, Fielding's own aristocratic tendencies make him argue for the largeness of heart and understanding which can come mainly from education and breeding, against his thesis that underlying character is merely modified in its expression, not basically altered, with social position; when he comes to *Amelia,* Atkinson is a tentative correction of this view.

The introductory remarks in *Tom Jones* set forth Fielding's intention of showing the effects of the country and city environments on the basic disposition and of organizing his novel as a comparative study of manners. As has been observed by many, he makes this plan basic to the formal structure of his novel: the first third of the book shows country behavior, the next the freer and more diversified characters of people on the road, and the last the false and circumscribed manners of fashionable society.

The vices of people of high position, he argues in the first section, appear also in everyone else, though in the lower orders they may be so embedded in violence as to escape immediate recognition. When Molly, for example, goes to church in the finery which Tom has given her, the consequence is the hilarious fight in the graveyard, because "The great are deceived if they imagine they have appropriated ambition and vanity to themselves. These noble qualities flourish as notably in a country church and churchyard as in the drawing-room or in the closet" (IV, vii). Aside from those vices apparently unrelated to class—lust, for example—the low also have their share of what might at first seem unsuitable snobbery. Molly's mother, a foul-mouthed slattern, is as proud to have been a clargyman's daughter, as is Mrs. Honour. Class molds the manner in which the disposition is manifested, but not the disposition itself.

After Molly has been discovered hiding the naked Square, her social inferiority and lack of sophistication are apparent: she lies in bed crying helplessly, because she is inexperienced, unlike the town lady who has "that perfection of assurance" which protects her on all occasions. In the middle of the book, Jenny Waters finds herself in a similar predicament at Upton, as does Lady Bellaston in the last section. (In the relative ages of the women, by the way, Fielding seems to be adjusting experience to the degree of corruption suitable to the country, the road, and the city.) Mrs. Waters cries "Rape" and "Murder," and faces out the discovery with the help of the landlady, who refuses to let her maid discuss the morals of gentry who pay substantial bills. Lady Bellaston is even more coolly self-sufficient: "without even looking at Jones [she] walked very majestically out of the room; there being a kind of dignity in the impudence of women of quality, which their inferiors vainly aspire to attain to in circumstances of this nature" (XV, vii). By comparison, Molly is almost innocent, as Fielding intends. He deliberately makes her animalistic, as he makes Squire Western animalistically irresponsible for his passions. Neither is depraved or concerned with manipulating others, unlike Lady Bellaston and her acquaintances.

In the violent and farcical class welter of the road, where officers may or may not be gentlemen, where village girls pass as captains' wives, barbers are former schoolmasters, servants act like great ladies, and inns are enchanted castles, only breeding and disposition are real. Tom, the apparent bastard, shows the courtesy and consideration of true gentility; Sophia, though a runaway, is a well-bred, kindly, unassuming lady; Fitzpatrick, who had charmed Mrs. Western and her fashionable niece at Brighton, a boor; Jenny Waters and Mrs. Fitzpatrick, despite differences in age and breeding, sisters in easy promiscuity. Only Squire Western, blissfully enclosed against all moral climates, is at all times the same chaos.

In London, Fielding complains that fashionable people are "so entirely made up of form and affectation, that they have no character at all, at least none which appears" (XIV, i). Moreover, the lower classes are misinformed if they think the upper one is at present lewd—fashionable women have been educated to think only of ambition and vanity, and therefore despise love, while their husbands are passionless ciphers. But the surface sterility can also mask vicious, self-enclosed passion: just as the lower orders of Somerset have all the high vices in crude form, so the nobility of London may be covering the most extreme and violent passions with superficial good manners. Worse, they are subject to the pervasive aristocratic delusion that their social inferiors are also inferior in the moral chain of being. Lady Bellaston, who is positively evil—i.e., purely selfish—under the veneer, tells Lord Fellamar to have Tom abducted by a press-gang: "Neither law nor conscience forbid this project; for the fellow, I promise you, however well dressed, is but a vagabond, and as proper as any fellow in the streets to be pressed into the service" (XVI, viii). She deliberately moves Tom into a lower class so that Fellamar, a sample cipher, should perceive him as nonhuman. Since the penalties for crimes by the nobility are trivial, an aristocrat with the courage to be self-enclosed, like Lady Bellaston, can do almost anything.

High society is therefore to be condemned for self-aggrandizement in the form of denying humanity to others, for triviality, and for a kind of monotonous sameness which in some is breeding and in others merely artificiality. In its judgment of humanity it tends to substitute formal and superficial criteria—fashionable manners, wealth, and display—for those based on human feeling. Middle society, by which Fielding on the whole means the untitled gentry, tends to be the finest, not having so much power with which to do evil. Wealthy members of this class, like All-worthy, may be excellent even with power—indeed, power gives them their chance to be excellent—because they are far enough away from the artificiality of London form, and because they have no one above them. But where such freedom may support an Allworthy, it also produces Westerns and, far worse, mad tyrants like the roasting squire of *Joseph Andrews*.

The lower orders, while they may have their virtues of plainness, honesty, sympathy, and so forth, have also a tendency toward savagery, gullibility, and, worst of all, the selfishness necessary in a world where their hold is tenuous. Servants and innkeepers (upper servants with all the faults of the others and an additional layer of bourgeois acquisitiveness) are the most thoroughly studied members of this class in the novel, since the focus of the work is on the world of their masters and patrons. And where Richardson tends to make his servants stereotypes of willing subordination, Fielding, out of a greater concern for both social realism and comedy, sees them in a constant battle for esteem and prerogatives, their loyalty primarily to themselves. It is very hard to be a generous, well-disposed servant.

Such competitiveness is the typical consequence of their position in the social order, whether they are individually well or ill disposed, whether their masters are considerate or disdainful. Allworthy's housekeeper Mrs. Wilkins, for example, is extremely obsequious to him and to anyone else of higher status than herself, while she at all times tyrannizes over her inferiors. In part, we are to understand that this is her nature. But since the combination of tyranny and servility appears also in Honour, in Mrs. Western's waiting woman, in Mrs. Slipslop of the earlier novel, and in most landladies, it is clearly central to Fielding's conception of the female upper servant. With women servants particularly, the superficial code of propriety—what Richardson's Pamela constantly calls her virtue—is never the admirable consequence of breeding but always a prudential acquisition not connected with the inner disposition. Like "prudence" for Blifil, "reason" for Square, and "religion" for Thwackum, "honor" or "character" for a serving woman is the formalized perversion of an attractive ideal.

Sophia's maid, Mistress Honour, is the most detailed study of this sort of self-righteous acquisitiveness in Fielding. When Sophia determines to run off, only her offers of great rewards can prevail over the various difficulties which Honour bases on her code of female propriety. But no sooner does Honour step out of her room than she begins to waver, Sophia's offer and her own fantasies of London on one side being countered by the presumption of a rich immediate reward from Western if she should betray her mistress' plans. She was still unsure how to act—and Fielding makes clear that she felt no gratitude, sympathy, even ordinary friendly concern for her mistress—when chance "sent an accident in her way, which at once preserved her fidelity, and even facilitated the intended business" (VII, viii): her self-importance was endangered. The deciding event was a hair-pulling match with Mrs. Western's maid about precedence, rank, and prestige.

When Honour storms drunkenly through an inn after hearing that the landlord thinks Sophia is Prince Charles's mistress, her pride is at the base of her resentment: "In proportion as the character of her mistress was raised, hers likewise, as she conceived, was raised with it; and, on the contrary, she thought the one could not be lowered without the other" (XI, viii). Similarly, Fielding points out, men servants are subject to the impressions created by their masters, though the qualities which society values in men are not moral but formal: men servants magnify the wealth and social positions of their masters, expecting these to affect their own prestige, but they have no concern for their moral or intellectual qualities. Servants thus think and judge like the most superficial abstraction of society, and are themselves judged largely by the reputation and behavior of others. Simply to assert their existence as human beings they need to be aggressive. Since society respects servants only in terms of their superiors' prestige, and since tenure with these superiors may be precarious, the worst self-seeking and self-enclosed aspects of their dispositions are fostered. The life of servants is the jungle life.

Like servants, innkeepers, more particularly landladies, are concerned only with what they can extract from the gentry. In theory, basic character is antecedent to environment but affected in its expression by environment: "there are certain characteristics in which most individuals of every profession and occupation agree. To be able to preserve these characteristics, and at the same time to diversify their operations, is one talent of a good writer" (X, i). But in practice Fielding expresses the general nature of innkeepers in a landlady's assumption that her husband would inform on Sophia as the notorious rebel Jenny Cameron, and in her willingness to shed a few tears at the execution of so pretty and courteous a lady. Despite theoretically possible exceptions, this is the normal pattern of landladies' actions. In socially formalized ways, servants and innkeepers are to do what is all mankind's duty—determine within oneself the attitudes, wishes, and psychological conditions of others. But the formalizing has degraded them, as it has degraded the ideas of prudence, reputation, reason, religion, love.

In *Amelia* class is a minor issue, much less significant, for example, than the relative importance of chance, character, and providence in the determination of destiny, or the effect of dominant passions on morality. Only two characters, Atkinson and Mrs. James, are notable as examinations of the relations between class and personality. In his treatment of Atkinson, Fielding experiments timidly with social mobility. Atkinson is from the beginning an extraordinarily noble member of the lower classes, who has acquired the ideals and the virtues of his superiors. When the Booths are desperate in Gibraltar, he offers to lend them all his money, demonstrating a generosity which no one in his position would have shown in *Tom Jones;* but Booth does not take the money, avoiding the equality that acceptance would have implied. Later, Atkinson is very awkward in the society of Mrs. Ellison's lodgers, never having learned to move gracefully, but he is so handsome that the women do not find him absurd. We discover eventually that he is the one who once stole the miniature of Amelia because he worshiped her, an action appropriate to an aristocratic lover, and he invariably acts nobly, kindly, loyally, honestly, bravely, courteously, and sympathetically, combining the virtues of both classes as Fielding had outlined them in his passage on conversation in *Tom Jones.* As a reward, Fielding does a thing which, as Orwell pointed out, Dickens would never chance, gives him a wife from the gentry; furthermore, Atkinson becomes a captain in the army. However, the wife is tainted, and so is the commission which she obtains for him improperly. There seems to be a certain ambiguity in his fate (though Fielding looks at him consistently enough), as if the author wanted to argue for the pre-eminence of character, but could not see how a noble member of the lower classes, given current English society, could achieve distinction in any pure way. If Joseph Andrews had not proved to be a gentleman by birth, only by the ambiguous actions of others could he have risen without compromising his own virtue.

As a study of what happens to an apparently attractive person in English upper society, Mrs. James becomes an emblem of that class. Mrs. James is a version of Lady Bellaston without the superadded menace or fantasy-spun sexuality: a cold society woman whose chief fault, as Fielding had written in *Tom Jones,* was triviality rather than lechery or a malicious will. However, her triviality entails an indifference to others which can cause as much harm as the most violent ill will. She plans to endanger Amelia as much as Lady Bellaston endangered Sophia, merely out of a wish to stay in London, where her predecessor wanted first a clear path to Jones and later revenge on him. In this way, and because of her relative realism, Mrs. James's apathetic corruption stands as a greater indictment of the current state of British society than the patently exaggerated and individual viciousness of Lady Bellaston. Mrs. James had become a woman "in whose opinion . . . outward form and ceremony constituted the whole essence of friendship: who valued all her acquaintance alike; as each individual served equally to fill up a place in her visiting roll; and who, in reality, had not the least concern for the good qualities or well-being of any of them" (V, iv). In short, her selfish coldness has so thoroughly deprived others of humanity that she has no humanity left herself. And such central coldness, in *Amelia,* is merely more susceptible to examination in the upper classes, not special to them. At the core of all the difficulties in England, Fielding by then sees a combination of selfishness and indifference which poisons the entire body of society, from the political lord who sneers at Harrison's zeal for reform to the Booths' maid, who runs off with Amelia's clothes.

But though the situation is bad, it is not hopeless, and from the beginning of his career to the *Journal of a Voyage to Lisbon* Fielding looked for a solution. He never found it, except in religion and in such segmental plans as enforcing wage ceilings, outlawing masquerades, limiting working holidays, strengthening penal laws, developing a metropolitan police force, and so on. The great achievement would have been, in the grand and classical manner, to develop a new scheme of education and thus improve the society by improving its citizens. Dr. Harrison's defense of human nature as basically good but perverted by education would suggest that Fielding had thought in this direction. However, Fielding is limited by his acceptance of the statically conceived system of society inherited from classical antiquity. Consequently, he takes for granted the traditional aims and paths of education, hopeful that if they are honorably sought, virtue will result. As Sherburn says, "Fielding seems to think of education as moral discipline rather than the acquisition of information or skill."[6]

The "Essay on the Knowledge of the Characters of Men" most fully deals with this sort of moral education, which inculcates both the ability to tell right from wrong and the sophistication to see the truth in human relations. The point of this essay, Fielding says, is to instruct the innocent good-hearted, who have so far indeed escaped corruption, but who at the same time cannot see reality. In this situation, instruction must be carefully distinguished from indoctrination; the former may supplement and protect the virtuous disposition, while the latter will replace it with machinery. For example, love usually expands outward from the self, through the immediate family, through neighbors, to the country, where it appears as patriotism. Such a process is good. In some places, however, as in Rome and Sparta, patriotism had been early and directly inculcated as a form of religion. Fielding disapproves of such thorough indoctrination, on the ground that it detracts from the psychological and moral freedom of the individual: "if 20 boys were taught from their infancy to believe that the Royal Exchange was the kingdom of heaven," nineteen of them would gladly sacrifice their lives for it as adults (*Works*, XIV, 303).

In everything that Fielding writes, he sees good breeding as primarily a moral quality, an indication of the mind's willingness to turn outward and to act for the good of others within the social sphere in which one has been placed. As a mainly comic artist, he presents this view largely through those who theoretically should be well bred but in fact are not. Informed that country squires are merely servants to their hunting dogs, his Don Quixote says, " 'Tis pity then that fortune should contradict the order of nature. It was a wise institution of Plato to educate children according to their minds, not to their births; these squires should sow that corn which they ride over. Sancho, when I see a gentleman on his own coach box, I regret the loss which some one has had of a coachman: the man who toils all day after a partridge or a pheasant, might serve his country by toiling after a plough; and when I see a low, mean, tricking lord, I lament the loss of an excellent attorney" (*Works*, XI, 18). Similarly, in *The Fathers* (which deals largely with the moral education of children), three spokesmen for virtuous good sense tell a fop just back from the grand tour that if he were systematically to cultivate the seeds of intelligence, he would be a tolerable suitor for the ingenue; he condemns the education which his coarse father gave him, and promises to try. While nothing can reform the innately evil, most people have some elements of good, and therefore can be taught their obligations in society and the fact that others exist. An education in good breeding could only turn the depraved squire of *Joseph Andrews* into a Blifil or a version of Mrs. Ellison's cousin; but given such better materials as Squire Western, it might have produced an idiosyncratic gentleman rather than a savage.

Though conventional breeding can do nothing to replace selfish with benevolent passions, it can modify or cover their weaker manifestations. Where the passionate Lady Booby's pride and lust are not involved, she can be perfectly courteous. In contrast to Lady Davers' violent response to Richardson's Pamela, in Fielding's correction of his competitor's portrayal of manners, Lady Booby surprises her nephew by her treatment of his new wife: "The lady received her with more civility than he expected; indeed, with the utmost: for she was perfectly polite, nor had any vice inconsistent with good breeding" (IV, iv). Wilson, narrating his troubles, sees a special kind of unpleasantness connected with class-determined bad breeding: "there is a malignity in the nature of man, which, when not weeded out, or at least covered by a good education and politeness, delights in making another uneasy or dissatisfied with himself." This weed, he says, is most evident among young people in "the lower classes of the gentry, and the higher of the mercantile world, who are, in reality, the worst-bred part of mankind" (III, iii). Though formal good breeding may lead to coldness, it prevents this sort of open viciousness.

In *Tom Jones,* manners are closely connected with class and situation, the differences between Squire Western and Mrs. Western being a fair indication of the effects of the latter, and those between Molly and Lady Bellaston of the effects of training, class, and age. Sophia, Fielding says, has been well educated in a private manner: though she lacks "a little of that ease in her behavior which is to be acquired only by habit, and living within what is called the polite circle, . . . yet its absence is well compensated by innocence; nor can good sense and a natural gentility ever stand in need of it" (IV, ii). Tom himself was similarly saved from fashionable affectation, though by the despicable Thwackum, and was kept innocent enough to be admirable. It took him a great while to realize that Sophia loved him: "To confess the truth, he had rather too much diffidence in himself, and was not forward enough in seeing the advances of a young lady, a misfortune which can be cured only by that early town education which is at present so generally in fashion" (V, ii). But he had an innate, or at least early developed, courtesy and openness of manner, which in action denoted good breeding.

Blifil, under the same tutelage, shows the gaucherie of the ill bred: at his formal visit to court Sophia there was a painful silence, "for the gentleman who was to begin the conversation had all the unbecoming modesty which consists in bashfulness" (VI, vii). The implication of the contrast with Tom and of the character of Atkinson in *Amelia* is that conversational ease is an expression of the good disposition, which can be helped by breeding and stunted by the manners of a lower class, but which can only be simulated after formal training by those who are not born with it. Had Blifil been bred in fashionable London, like Lord Fellamar, he could have given the empty illusion of fluent conversation without feeling the sympathy which underlay Tom's manner. Fitzpatrick, for example, with the skill though not the disposition, was enabled to deceive his wife and her aunt, both of whom followed the fashionable rules rather than the heart: as his wife said of him, "it requires a most penetrating eye to discern a fool through the disguises of gaiety and good breeding" (XI, v).

A good education in manners is, therefore, an aid also to morality, in that it represses overt selfishness and assumes at least an intellectual awareness of the humanity of others. In the *Journal*, Fielding describes how he found himself the butt of nasty jokes from sailors and watermen as, visibly ill, he was with difficulty carried on board the ship. Such barbarism, he thinks, is confined to the English, and with them to the lowest class: "it is an excrescence of an uncontroul'd licentiousness mistaken for liberty, and never shews itself in men who are polish'd and refin'd, in such manner as human nature requires, to produce that perfection of which it is susceptible, and to purge away that malevolence of disposition, of which, at our birth we partake in common with savage creation" (*Journal*, p. 45). Good breeding, then, is a training in civilization, leading men out of brutality. Mankind is not by its very nature divided into classes. Character qualities of all sorts are spread among men with no regard to class, but good education—normally available only to the upper classes—either rubs the bad qualities down to a minimum or hides them from view. A good education, when combined with a good disposition, leads to the highest type of human being; good formal learning is quite secondary to good breeding, as witness the relatively unlearned Allworthy, the most admirable figure in Fielding.

Though Fielding rarely discusses the techniques of education, he does elaborate on one issue, which had been important to Locke (and treated at great length by Richardson's Pamela in her adaptation of Locke's *Some Thoughts Concerning Education*): private tutoring as against public schools for boys, as well as the complementary pattern for young men, the university as against the grand tour or fashionable life. When Adams asserts that Wilson's troubles derived from his public school, Joseph, claiming to echo his late master Sir Thomas Booby, answers that public schools provide excellent experience, "for great schools are little societies, where a boy of any observation may see in epitome what he will afterwards find in the world at large" (III, v). Adams, inconsistent with his theoretical focus on outgoing courage and charity, urges that very reason for preferring a private school, under a tutor, since he wants to protect the boys' "innocence and ignorance." The often quoted reply by Joseph again brings us to Fielding's assumptions about predisposition. Boys, he says, may be just as vicious in a private school, as witness many squires: "in the stable, if a young horse was vicious in his nature, no correction would make him otherwise; I take it to be equally the same among men: if a boy be of a mischievous, wicked inclination, no school, though ever so private, will ever make him good, on the contrary, if he be of a righteous temper, you may trust him in London, or wherever else you please—he will be in no danger of being corrupted" (III, v). As if to support Joseph, the depraved squire who is lord of misrule had been educated at home, under "a tutor who had orders never to correct him, nor to compel him to learn more than he liked," and had returned from a tour of the continent "with a hearty contempt for his own country; especially what had any savour of the plain spirit and honesty of our ancestors" (III, vii). Though Fielding returned to the topic from time to time, he did not firmly support either Joseph's or Adams's views.[7] He could not repudiate either the enclosed virtues or the excursion into danger; and no single method could suitably educate mankind's varying dispositions.

Fielding's lack of interest in the form of education—another kind of superficial machinery—is evident in *Tom Jones*. Allworthy had Tom and Blifil educated at home to escape the vices of the public schools, under a devout, upright clergyman and a secular moral philosopher. Adams would have approved, but when we are shown Thwackum and Square, the personalities with whom the boys are closely confined, we wonder how much worse public education could have been. Furthermore, under such masters one boy escapes vices while the other has learned enough hypocrisy to nurture them all. The only conclusion is a shrug of the shoulders. Such a master as Thwackum will train people evilly wherever he is, and such a student as Blifil will be a villain despite whatever is taught him. Partridge conducts a village school, to which some children of a local squire are sent: a fool is charged, in innocence and ignorance, with teaching dolts. Following another path, Allworthy himself "had missed the advantage of a learned education," but had taught himself so diligently and had so well profited by talking with eminent scholars "that he was himself a very competent judge in most kinds of literature" (I, x). Here, Fielding seems to be implying that a man of native intelligence and good disposition can learn for himself what a university provides for its students. Surely, Allworthy everywhere speaks in an educated and liberal manner; but the passage specifically prepares for his patronage of the corrupt Dr. Blifil. Untaught integrity, then, is sufficient for virtue, but may contribute to one's being imposed on. Yet Dr. Blifil was genuinely learned. We can conclude again that no system can guarantee a knowledge of men, while a knowledge of books is to be gained in many ways. Perhaps for this reason Fielding provides each of his heroes with an older guard: Adams, Allworthy, Harrison. Only experience, wisely interpreted, can save good people amidst the murk of society.

In the *Covent-Garden Journal* Fielding's growing conservatism leads to stronger objections to current education. In the good old days, he says, young men were sent to schools or universities, where they were shielded from the world; now, at fifteen or sixteen they are taken to London, where they learn all the corrupt practices, and are either perfected in corruption on the grand tour (*CGJ*, II, 3-4) or brought home to become rustic boobies (*CGJ*, II, 65-66). Those who go on to the university may learn if they wish or indulge in corruptions if they wish. But "This is a Matter which I shall handle very tenderly, as I am clearly of an Opinion that an University Education is much the best we have; for here at least there is some Restraint laid on the Inclinations of our Youth" (*CGJ*, II, 66). At this point and for the only time, Fielding apparently favors university education; but the reason, as in Cowper's *Tirocinium,* is purely its disciplinary efficiency. Education for Fielding is not the acquisition of knowledge, though he can be as loftily contemptuous as Gibbon of the lack of classical learning. In addition to revealing the nature of human society, education is valuable primarily as a curb on the selfishness of the passionate upper classes, as an infusion of sympathetic imagination.

Observing human character in its environment, Fielding believes with such writers as Swift, Pope, and Johnson that an artificial social order is necessary to prevent undue social competition and its consequent pain. He never claims that aristocrats are innately better than their social inferiors; but he wishes society to behave as if they were, so that the life of society can be carried on with a minimum of friction. Ideally, the aristocracy is to do the guarding, the governing, the thinking, and the moral posturing for the nation, in company with the gentry; the commercial class is to direct fruitful and necessary trade and industry; and the lower orders are to work.

But decay has set in, largely because the increase of trade and the consequent increase in the power of money have fomented a spirit of independence in the common people. In Plato's terms, the appetites are ruling the mind of the state. The upper orders have been corrupted through the introduction of luxury (a consequence of the spread of trade) and their partial displacement by the power of money. Luxury has seeped downward, encouraging the baser passions of the multitude through the lure of satisfying them; with controls lax, selfishness is rewarded. The cure is restriction upon the lower people, since they are somewhat less corrupt than the upper, since their work is most directly useful in maintaining the existence of the state, and since they alone are weak enough to be restricted. If the state's disposition has been to a certain extent stifled by the ineffectiveness of the aristocracy, Fielding seems to be hoping that at least the senses, the elementary qualities which maintain contact with the outer world, may be purified. If the lower orders can be brought back to some awareness of their proper functions, they will be available for good use when the upper classes resume responsibility.

A very great danger in the division of society is the self-enclosure of its constituent parts. Noblemen cannot understand the misery of poverty, so that both their interest in helping its victims and their own moral improvement—even when they are willing to be improved—are improperly limited. As Booth says, even well-intentioned great men "have no perfect idea of those common distresses of mankind which are far removed from their own sphere. Compassion, if thoroughly examined, will, I believe, appear to be the fellow-feeling only of men of the same rank and degree of life for one another, on account of the evils to which they themselves are liable" (X, ix). Similarly, the wealthy fail to sympathize with any goals not attainable through money. The lower classes, among them the boatmen who mock the sick Fielding, have been so habituated to grub for life and to satisfy their gross appetites that they understand no motives but selfish ones. Only the middling gentry, like Allworthy and Wilson, away from the anonymity of the city, can be trained to respond to the needs of others with actions which can psychologically reward themselves. And even this class, as witness Western and the squire in *Joseph Andrews,* is in danger of being self-enclosed by passions. The noble and the rich, too often letting their responsibilities lapse under the general cascade of luxury, tend to wallow within self-enclosed privileges, reducing their inferiors to things and overwhelming their country's laws. All three of the major classes are bursting all limitations, making a shapeless mass of the ideal pyramid of the state. In *Amelia,* Fielding seems in full retreat, finding virtue possible only in the occasional mind, not in society.

In such a society, the writer who believes in the existence of virtuous individuals and in widespread but uncultivated good seeds has a clear function. If he can write fiction, he is to range among the classes, communicating with basic humanity at every level and interpreting the accidental variations induced by level, so that all readers may be made aware of both the substance and the accidents. To a considerable extent, Fielding's novels have the aim of showing how social position—environment—can alter the surface and sometimes, through encouragement of some qualities and repression of others, the total configuration of character. A novel such as *Tom Jones* serves the highest purpose of forcing awareness of varied humanity upon its readers. The author and the hero have ventured out into the world to do good and to exhibit its results—Fielding in his novel and Tom in his harmonious mind. And all the novels, as educational devices, are aimed at the same target as the essays, the social tracts, the early poems, and the plays: the revelation of the reality of the surrounding world, so that the reader may interact humanely with it. Besides all their other artistic aims, the novels are to constitute the wise and experienced guidance which every reader of good will needs for his own life in society.

VI

Fantasy and Actuality

DESPITE FIELDING'S HOPES for reform and the buoyancy of *Joseph Andrews* and *Tom Jones,* his novels often have sad implications, as is inevitable when happiness is seen as residing only within the mind. He provides us with gloriously triumphant fantasies—the deliberate substitution of the ideal for the actual— but frequently forces us to abandon them, or at least subordinate them to sane awareness of surrounding actuality. Pervasively, he opposes the romance, the fairy tale, the myth or reverie, the self-indulgence of the mind, with the actuality which seems to give it the lie.[1]

Sometimes the actuality is dramatically active; sometimes it is strongly implied. In the jolliest book, *Joseph Andrews,* the checks of reality are relatively minor, though too evident to overlook. Actuality is more insistent in the other novels. In *Tom Jones* Fielding's comment on the tendency of some to substitute what they would like to see for what exists implies his own contrasting intentions: "There are a set of religious, or rather moral writers, who teach that virtue is the certain road to happiness, and vice to misery, in this world. A very wholesome and comfortable doctrine, and to which we have but one objection, namely, that it is not true." Real virtue, he says, is likely in this world to reap "poverty and contempt, with all the mischiefs which backbiting, envy, and ingratitude can bring on mankind," and sometimes jail (XV, i). While Fielding, writing comedy, necessarily shows virtue rewarded in this life and vice and folly curbed, he makes sure at every step that we see the normal probabilities. Tom very nearly committed incest and murder; Sophia is very nearly married by force to a villain. Captain Blifil *did* marry Allworthy's sister; Western's brutality *did* destroy his wife. Without Fielding's self-conscious interference, we are to understand that a person in Tom's position would be irrevocably lost (as Molière, one of Fielding's models, makes it clear that without a royal miracle a decent family could never overcome a monster of hypocrisy).[2] In *Amelia*, the implications become explicit.

Everything by Fielding, no matter how prosaic or fantastic, has as one function the illumination of what he conceived to be the actual conditions and constituents of human nature and society. As usual, the lesser works give good hints of the ways in which he juxtaposes fantasy and actuality in the major novels. In the *Journey from This World to the Next,* for example, the whole series of incarnations of Julian the Apostate, in itself a conception of pure fantasy derived from Lucian, is handled with the techniques of realism, as Julian reaps the various consequences of his various moral characteristics. To cite one career almost at random, Julian was once a young man who fell in love with a girl not rich enough "to justify my marriage with her, in the opinion of the wise and prudent." After a painful struggle, he gave her up, since "I could by no means prevail with myself to sacrifice that character of profound wisdom, which I had with such uniform conduct obtained, and with such caution hitherto preserved" (*Works,* II, 276). While he quibbled, she married someone else, leaving him to marry a rich widow and be miserable. His life was doomed to hypocrisy, for he abandoned many pleasures and enjoyed others secretly, all for the reputation of wisdom and gravity. As with many notable uses of the exotic in the mid-century—*Rasselas,* or Goldsmith's "Asem," or Smollett's *Adventures of an Atom*—the consequences of the major improbabilities in plot are developed in terms of social and psychological actuality in eighteenth-century England.

Jonathan Wild, insofar as it is not a moral or political allegory, is pure fantasy, with the implications of actual life spelled out in exaggerated ways: instead of merely deploring the success of rascality when it attacks innocence, Fielding elaborates it into a burlesque of the sentimental drama. Not only is Heartfree robbed of all his money, but he is accused of swindling, his wife is induced to leave him, and he is condemned to death. The characters are so clearly caricatures of actuality that we do not object to ingenious plot reversals which bring the Heartfrees out of difficulties and Wild into them, and we join in Fielding's delight at his brazen adroitness. No realistic course which threatens virtue is allowed to proceed to its normal end; and the situation is likely to be absurd, as in Mrs. Heartfree's hilarious adventures. Similarly, Heartfree's reprieve, in the conscious burlesque of traditional form which is a major mode of the book, is deliberately delayed to the last moment, and deliberately advertised to the reader for what it is, a miraculous evasion of implied reality: "lest our reprieve should seem to resemble that in the Beggars' Opera, I shall endeavor to show him that this incident, which is undoubtedly true, is at least as natural as delightful; for we assure him we would rather have suffered half mankind to be hanged than have saved one contrary to the strictest rules of writing and probability" (IV, vi). That we are to compare the events and characters of *Jonathan Wild* with actual life, and be warned by the villain's maxims, is fairly clear. But what we are to understand as the nature of the real world is not. We can see well enough that Wild and what he stands for are dangerous and vile, but without the discussion of greatness and goodness in the preface to the *Miscellanies* we could not tell what to make of the Heartfrees or how to deal with aggressive evil in the actual world. The superb irony seems to be indulged in for its own sake as much as for our enlightenment.

In the preface to *Joseph Andrews*, Fielding regretfully asserts the impossibility of staying within the limits of comic fantasy if the constituents of it are to be people as one knows them in life. Though follies are the proper substance of the ridiculous, the vices inevitable in drawing "nature" are too serious for amusement. Despite his assurances that these vices will not triumph, the novel itself inescapably implies that without authorial intervention virtue would be destroyed. In London, Joseph's fellow-servants at once subject him to temptation, and though he resists pretty well, he dresses gaudily and participates in theater riots; ideal as Joseph's appearances before us show him to be, Fielding implies that the actual condition of being a footman forbids completely virtuous behavior. On the road at night after Joseph has been dismissed, he is robbed, beaten, stripped, and tossed into a ditch for dead. Through the element of romance, "story," a coach stops after his groans are heard, and again we see that normally the postilion would overlook the groans, or, if he were kind and adventurous, that the passengers would insist on driving past. We are to understand that an actual person in Joseph's situation would die.

The grimness of the alternatives to fantasy is communicated largely through implication in *Joseph Andrews,* since in that novel Fielding is not concerned to work out as limiting a series of events as in *Tom Jones,* where he insists on giving us "natural" situations and complications. That is, the first novel is much more than the others the fairy-tale adventures of odd, even unique people, highly exaggerated over whatever living models they could be based on. At the beginning, Joseph is a male version of what Fielding believes to be a wildly improbable character, Richardson's Pamela. The delightful Adams is an intellectual conception of the combination of perfect active goodness with complete innocence. Fanny, like Gilbert's Patience, is a caricature of the quintessential milkmaid. In their actions in the plot, they do not have the moral significance of typicality or presumed normality. The encounter between Joseph and the predatory Mrs. Slipslop early in the novel means no more than a good joke, whereas the reactions of Tom in similar situations have evident moral implications about the behavior of inexperienced but good-natured youth when faced with sexual temptation. Joseph's beauty so powerfully affects Betty the chambermaid (who is as much Cervantes' Maritornes as she is Good Samaritan) that he is forced to throw her out of the room to protect his chastity—a burlesque of Pamela's troubles, a deliberately exaggerated fantasy of male attractiveness, but not an exemplum. Tom Jones, a much less fabulous hero, attracts the promiscuous Molly and Jenny, but both engagements are affected by his social position, and both reflect his moral nature and his realistic opportunity to choose. Booth, in the last novel, is brought into Miss Matthews' bed after a long train of circumstances that provide her actions with a context and an analysis of her character that makes the result likely. Fielding moves steadily from a novel in which exaggeration implies the realistic alternative to one in which not only the possible but the probable and perhaps even the inevitable take place, according to his late view that a life is a consistent pattern of actions.[3]

In *Joseph Andrews* the contrast between the likely danger of the outer world of action and the self-enclosed world of fantasy is epitomized in the adventures of the heroes and the leisurely journey of Lady Booby's entourage, which Fielding makes available for indifferent rescues. When Joseph is held hostage for the feed bill for Adams' horse, Mrs. Slipslop conveniently comes along to pay his ransom. At another time, Peter Pounce's coach saves Fanny from certain rape and the men from an embarrassing and possibly dangerous imprisonment. While Joseph, Fanny, and Adams are properly brave and buoyant in their travels through the English countryside, the natives (acting on the selfish principles of "nature") are not generally friendly, and the actual workings of the social system are most threatening.[4] A real trip of this sort would certainly end in exploitation or prison, and possibly in death. If the journey epitomizes the movement out of the self into right action in the world, Fielding makes no guarantees of easy success. The only assured reward is internal.

Even the inserted Leonora romance, which in the tradition Fielding inherited from Cervantes would be divorced from its realistic context, is at times used for direct or implied comment on social actuality. During one of its interruptions, Miss Grave-Airs, a prudish passenger, refuses to allow the limping Joseph to ride in the same coach with her because he is a footman, the sort of treatment which he might have met regularly outside a novel. An exchange between Adams and the narrator sharply indicates the stupidity and ignorance of judges of courts of sessions. In the romance itself, when Leonora's father avariciously refuses to give Bellarmine a fortune with her, he abandons his suit and runs off to Paris, she immures herself in a lonely great house, and Horatio, staying a bachelor, soberly sticks to business and grows rich. Again, Leonora's aunt seems much more appropriate to a satire on society than to a romantic tale: she urges Leonora to break her word to Horatio for the sake of a richer match, has taken bribes, and is a religious hypocrite. All of this is dismayingly realistic for a romantic insert, in which we might expect at least a suicide or two for love. Compare, for example, the heroics in the inserted tales in *Don Quixote*, Fielding's model.[5]

To allow for this pervasive contrasting of the actual with the fabulous, Fielding arranges for Adams not to keep his clerical gown clean or, at times, even visible; consequently, he can be involved in uncensored English life of a sort that might not be available to an actual pastor in full bloom. In their first contact with the legal system, Adams, Joseph, and Fanny are saved by pure luck, an indication of what their fates might have been in the ordinary course of life. Only the coincidental presence of a gentleman who recognized Adams saved him and Fanny from commitment on the spot by an ordinary justice of the peace. Without help from the gentry, such poor as depart from the normal—a man in a dirty cassock accompanied by a disheveled dairy maid, for example—are in danger from Fielding's society.

From time to time, as in the discussion of the quarter-session, the contrasts are made overtly. After a congenial innkeeper damns the false-promising squire (a conscious and therefore dishonest Don Quixote) and cites the damage that he has done, Adams observes that since he has the appearance in his face of "that sweetness of disposition, which furnishes out a good Christian," he may still reform (II, xvii). The host argues that this is nonsense. If one has traveled in the world, he says, the only thing one expects to learn from a stranger's face is whether he has had the smallpox. Adams, at this point absurd, heatedy pursues his argument that the classics teach more about human character than does experience. Just in time to prevent violence, Joseph arrives, to demonstrate again the deliberate doubleness of Fielding's view. In the normal course of the argument, Adams would have seriously annoyed the host, who surely would have revoked his cheerful assumption of the cost of their meals as an unrecoverable debt. The best of men, if he is eccentric and therefore enclosed against others on certain issues, will alienate even his friends in the actual world.

In the background of the jolly events, but visible to all of us, is the immense danger in which the poor in England find themselves, the immense power of the squires. A young neighbor shoots the harmless dog of Wilson's daughter, and there is nothing to be done about it. The vicious squire who captures the wandering trio on the hare hunt is angry over the damage done by Joseph and Adams; and while he and his lackeys ponder what to do we realize that they can do practically anything. The actions of the squire take the form of folly and practical jokes—an indication of the triviality to which idleness and power and ignorance lead—but he also organizes the abduction of Fanny and the beating of her escorts. He and his "curs" are available for any viciousness, and are consequently utterly dangerous to any weaker people, who have no recourse against them without the unlikely help of Peter Pounce and his men.

Pounce's hypocritical fantasy about the wastefulness of charity in such a mild and fertile land as England is another crisp indication of the difference between the dream as some would like it and the actuality. We know that he lies, and so does Adams, who soon leaves the coach. But his argument is no more absurd than the continual rescuing of the main characters, which equally forces on us the contrasting truth. Lady Booby's threats to turn Adams from his curacy if he publishes the bans for Joseph's wedding a second time again point up the conflict of actuality and fantasy. Adams, as he must, says that he cannot deviate from the church's rules no matter what the cost, and the novel is so arranged that her threat is not carried out. But we know that actually he and his family are at her mercy. Lest we miss the point, Fielding earlier had him tell us that all his hopes for preferment had been destroyed time and again by his refusal to sell his nephew's vote at elections. Moreover, while his courageous stands indicated his integrity and contributed to his mental peace, their beneficiaries in a corrupt system were as bad as his tempters. The political actuality was shameful, perhaps hopeless; the only good was in the ideal political myths in Adams's mind.

At the end, all the complications are settled miraculously and happily, as they should be in a comic epic. But the effect is different from, say, a Roman comedy, where a number of implausible, stylized people run through a plot which is not a comment on contemporary life even though it exhibits a good many "realistic" details and the issues (marriage, the freeing of a slave, the son's rebellion against the father) are part of everyday life. *Joseph Andrews* also differs significantly from such English versions of the classical comic tradition as Jonson's *Alchemist* and *Bartholomew Fair*. In those, the characters and their actions are primarily comments on the consequence of folly and vice; while everything is providentially made right in the end, there has been no danger for decent, good-natured, reasonable people like ourselves. All we need do is mind our business and avoid the complacent folly of Littlewit or the wild pride of Sir Epicure Mammon and we will be all right. In contrast, all the fortuitous escapes of the central trio in *Joseph Andrews*, as well as the breakneck plotting of the conclusion, persuade us that without the conscious intervention of the author our chances of survival, if we were in their place, would not be good. The fantasy and the actuality comment on each other. Outer actuality—which must be faced—can very possibly be murderous. In an escape to the fantastic lies some safety; but one cannot always live in fantasy (or an ideal estate in the country). Adams can reason in the purity of his mind wherever he is. But less saintly figures like Joseph, Fanny, and pre-eminently Wilson, must demonstrate the goodness of their dispositions in the world before they can retire to serenity.

Tom Jones is much less concerned with opposing fantasy and reality than *Joseph Andrews,* since its aim is not specifically to expose affectation and vanity—i.e., the contrast between the actuality and the ideal that we attempt to indulge or that others attempt to impose on us. Rather, Fielding's goal is to portray our lives: "The provision, then, which we have here made is no other than Human Nature." While it is not pervasively a moral allegory, the second novel has specific aims for which plot and character have to be fused in a context of probability, so that moral choices will make sense as consequences of character patterns.

The realistic alternatives to ideal actions are usually not merely implied; they are generally stated, and good reasons are given when they are not chosen. When Allworthy determines to keep the baby, at least until the parents can be found, Mrs. Wilkins shows us that one might easily leave it at the churchwarden's door to take its meager chances of surviving the storm. But the character of Allworthy is such that the fantasy act of bringing up the child as his own is probable: there are generous squires in England, everyone knows him to be such a squire, and someone of his character is very likely to raise the child. Furthermore, we later discover that the mother is his own sister, who surely knows him well enough to expect this benevolence. The question of Partridge's punishment for fathering an illegitimate child again shows the basic difference between the novels. Where any of the justices in the first would have consigned him to a bridewell at the slightest suggestion that he was guilty, Allworthy is brought a good deal of information to this effect before he acts, and then his action is merely banishment. Compare with these events the first rescue of Joseph Andrews by the accidentally well-disposed postilion of a coach which happens to be passing by, and the difference is obvious. Formally, the good people's adventures are no longer ruled by chance, but are determined by their own characters interacting with a normally systematized world.

This is not to say that Fielding has completely abandoned so effective a technique as the implied contrast of fantasy and actuality. It is used beautifully in the famous chapter in which Captain Blifil dies (II, viii). In the course of that chapter, the Captain has been plotting in some detail the mistreatment of everyone in sight as soon as he should inherit Allworthy's vast fortune—and it is likely that he should outlive Allworthy, who is considerably older. But the Captain dies suddenly of apoplexy, and the threat has become a fantasy which is casually blown away. However, this sudden death is by no means as unlikely as the appearance of Peter Pounce's men just in time to prevent Fanny's irretrievable ruin. Given the Captain's choleric temper and the complex psychological strains under which he has been living, it is perfectly plausible, in Fielding's terms, that he should die at this age, while Allworthy's goodness and serenity give him a fair chance of long life. Furthermore, death comes to the Captain while he is alone, and he is generally an isolated man, concerned only with himself and viewing all society as his enemy. Allworthy is later gravely ill, but since he is a social person eager to spread good around him, he is surrounded by people (at least two of whom, Tom and the doctor, want to help him), and he receives the necessary attention. In short, Fielding here uses something of the old technique to suggest the plight in which the good people might be if he had not supplied an alternative, but the event which he does provide is credible—possible, and often probable —and not solely fantasy.

Similarly, Honour's vacillation over whether to betray Sophia's plan to run away suggests to us that in actuality, if Fielding were not pulling strings, Sophia would probably be forced into marriage with Blifil. As various critics have observed, the story of the Man of the Hill is also what might, and in some ways surely would, happen to Tom if he were not saved by Fielding's intervention. Again, the moral autobiography of Mrs. Fitzpatrick shows the possibilities for Sophia if she runs off to be married or if she is forced to marry a detestable man.[6] In general, while the combination of happiness and virtue is a possible goal in Fielding's scheme, he finds that except through comic dispensation it is very rarely achieved. But at the same time he is careful to ground his choices in what he has shown to be character: Honour is confirmed as Sophia's by her own contentious nature; the Man of the Hill has trusted worse people than has Tom and lacks Tom's selfless, outgoing spirits; and Mrs. Fitzpatrick has always been flightier than her cousin.

As the novel reaches London the unsatisfactory alternatives— the actuality as against the engaging fantasy—are more frequently made to occur or more powerfully suggested. Mrs. Miller, the kindly landlady with whom Tom stays in London, exercises a firm authority over her children which, since it is always for their good, they readily obey. She is thus, like the gypsy king, followed out of love, and very unlike the many other parents in the novel who quarrel with their children on the subject of marriage. In requital, her obedient daughter becomes pregnant anyway. Nancy is saved from destruction—and Fielding is at considerable pains to show how likely it is that Nightingale would actually desert her— through the good offices of Tom Jones and Fielding, and through the weak goodness of Nightingale's character, which allows Tom to persuade him. This episode touches on the sordid, and Tom's relations with Lady Bellaston seem even grimier. Lady Bellaston is middle-aged, she has an unpleasant smell, and she gives Tom money, three extremely unromantic considerations which suggest the direction in which Tom might be forced if it were not for his basically moral nature and the devices by which Fielding saves him. But the two are equally important. If Tom were incapable of realizing his faults, if he could not easily resist solving his money problems by marrying the succulent Widow Hunt, Fielding's devices would be useless. Though no system can successfully anticipate the oddities of human whim or the accidents in which the world abounds, a mind which wishes to cultivate its own good seeds can prevail over circumstance. Fielding is firmly and seriously in control of the moral significance of plot and character in *Tom Jones,* as he did not yet wish to be in *Joseph Andrews.*

Though one can argue that the sentimental rules which seem to affect the emotions of various characters in *Amelia* at various times are a considerable distance away from actuality, nonetheless the novel is concerned with a greater realism than are its predecessors.[7] Throughout the novel, the poverty of the hero's family is the direct result of his maladjustment in a sordid world. Specifically, Booth is introduced at his trial before Justice Thrasher, for having come to the rescue of a man attacked by two others. The assailants bribe the constable and are let off, but Booth and the man he helped are jailed because they have no money. Here the hero suffers the consequences of the social situation which Fielding describes, whereas in *Joseph Andrews* the admirable figures are saved in exactly the same situations, and in *Tom Jones* they are explicitly kept out of similar dangers. The legal and social systems and human nature are the same in all three novels; but Fielding varies the ways in which they interact so that the tones of the novels are different.

Grotesquerie—"humour"—is minimized in *Amelia,* as domestic tragi-comedy takes the place of burlesque and comedy. Booth, successfully farming Harrison's land, bought an old coach and a harness, and immediately became an object of envy and hatred to his neighbors, who conspired to ruin him: an echo of the response to Molly Seagrim's fancy clothes and to Jenny Jones's learning, but without the burlesque violence of the earlier novel. The Methodist pickpocket and the deist gambler, both of whom manage to cheat Booth in prison, are essentially Thwackum and Square reduced to the operative meanness of ordinary life. The prison warden, who conspires with Miss Matthews, is "the governor of the enchanted castle" (IV, i) where Booth is lured into adultery, and with the phrase Fielding directly implies the difference between the romantic notion (reinforced by suggestions of the Circe episode and, as Fielding said elsewhere, of Dido and Aeneas) and the sordid reality. But the narrative here, as against the earlier novels, is of two flawed people in prison, not of heroes in fairy tales. Sentiment, in the sense of calling forth sympathy by dwelling on the sad family consequences of such flaws as gambling and philandering, is dominant. But so far as possible, the sentimental which forgives chronic sinfulness is avoided. The change and growth of Mrs. James's character, while at times implausible and inconsistent, depend on more "realistic" considerations of environment than, for example, the deathbed repentance of Square. And sordid actuality comes with a melodramatic vengeance in the denouement of Mrs. Bennet's story: not only does her flirtatious innocence lead to sexual exploitation by the lord, but she is further punished by a venereal infection—a drastic step beyond what happens to anyone (except, in his distant and emblematic past, to Wilson) in the first two novels.

Fielding's miraculous intervention is useful in providing the happy ending, as it had been in the first two novels, but before that point fantasy is relatively minor in the plot and tone. Lawyer Murphy and Amelia's sister are fortunately discovered as the villains who substituted a false will, and Booth and Amelia are extricated from their troubles. However, Dr. Harrison's return to England had guaranteed at least a tolerable haven if their debts remained low enough for him to assume, and the demonstration of Booth's incompetence to deal with social actuality can be cut short at any stage of the novel. I do not want to suggest that the wildly suitable poetic justice which affects everyone at the end of the novel is more realistic than the conclusion of *Tom Jones*. But even Blifil, an unambiguous rogue, was treated leniently in the earlier novel; here, however, the fairly well-disposed thief Robinson seems reformed, "after which he returned to vicious courses, took a purse on the highway, was detected and taken" and hanged: "So apt are men whose manners have been once thoroughly corrupted, to return, from any dawn of an amendment into the dark paths of vice" (XII, ix). In the last novel, Fielding surely wishes to deal more directly than before with habit, with character, with the squalor of the social system, and with the severe punishments provided by man and human nature. Most of the symbolic action is in the external world, which is a welter of ambiguities.

The myths or fantasies which Fielding employs for his comments on reality are of various sorts, appropriate to their various functions in the novels. The most simple are within the minds of the characters, as for example Adams' confusion of reality with scripture or classical literature, or Captain Blifil's dreams of vast expense and tyrannical rule, or Colonel James's of the pleasures of sexual dalliance. These illuminate the essence of the characters and do much to explain motivation and action. Of another sort are the deliberate falsifications of character which Fielding describes as romantic and which he delights in contrasting with actuality, as in his exposure of the hypocrisy of Richardson's Pamela through the burlesque experiences of her brother at the beginning of *Joseph Andrews*.

Less obvious, but more fundamental in the development of the novels, are the archetypal experiences with which Fielding himself seems to be preoccupied, at least so far as to use them recurrently and signally. Such archetypes are not strictly fantasies, as I have so far used the term, since they do not necessarily represent an ideal deliberately provided as a contrast to actuality. But even in the terms of Fielding's time, and surely in those of ours, distinctions between the wish and the perception cannot be sharply made; rather, the false wish (a footman's pious chastity) and the sordid actuality (the depravity of Londoners) are extremes. On the continuum between them, archetypes are closer to fantasy than to actuality; they are patterned conceptions introduced into chaotic actuality—the fundamental elements of plot, which gives shape to possible events.

One such archetype, which has been mentioned or implied in a good deal that has gone before, is the confrontation of relatively simple innocence with the varied and confusing experience of the world. Sometimes the character is thereby educated, as is true of Tom Jones and Wilson and partially of Booth. Tom learns how to act in the world, but then confines himself to the microcosm of the country as soon as he can. Booth learns little, unless his conversion to Christianity is educational; but Fielding does not adequately demonstrate the conversion, perhaps because Booth's nature as it has been developed cannot be permanently stabilized. Sometimes the confrontation leads to the reader's enlightenment though not the character's, as witness Adams, the Man of the Hill, and Heartfree.

In *Jonathan Wild* Fielding presents most baldly the conflict of evil in the protagonist with the completely innocent goodness of the Heartfrees. Heartfree's innocence is static and passive: existing virtuously within a narrow sphere, he does not move out seeking to do good in the world. He seems to live only to be imposed on, and we can understand his victimization as symbolic rather than realistic. As the preface to the *Miscellanies* implies, Fielding here sees innocence as goodness and a reliance on cynical "reality" (one simple expression of experience) as "greatness," preferring goodness enlightened by an awareness of reality. In the book itself, however, Fielding's treatment of the Heartfrees is ambiguous, as it is of the contemporaneous Parson Adams. While he always hated self-enclosed evil, Fielding at this point also has some of the man-of-the-world's contempt for the completely innocent.

The author's ambiguity appears in the Joseph of the early chapters,[8] whose ridiculous devotion to chastity cannot be taken seriously, and in the character of Adams. Adams is immensely learned, sensible, and kind, but "as entirely ignorant of the ways of this world as an infant just entered into it could possibly be" (I, iii). And Adams is not wholly admirable in his innocence, or at least we are surely not supposed to emulate him in the absurdity which accompanies his moral attractiveness. When Adams tells the bookseller how badly he needs to sell his manuscript sermons, Fielding squarely faces the reader with the incompatibility of business—concentrated selfishness—and Christianity. But while we are to despise the bookseller for his selfish insensitivity, we cannot admire Adams for attempting to engage in an activity which he thoroughly misunderstands. More seriously, Adams prefers private to public schools precisely because they protect the boys' "innocence and ignorance," thereby suggesting one of the tangents by which one world of fantasy can meet reality. In the world of moral fantasy, innocence can be eternally maintained, while in social England its only equivalent is ignorance. In one lucid moment, Adams is aware that the two go together, and is willing to settle for them in combination. This is a considerable step forward from his insistence to the innkeeper that the characters of real people can be learned through studies of physiognomy and classical literature.

Tom Jones is primarily a *bildungsroman* tracing the growth and education of a well-disposed youth; but it also exhibits the innocence of others in the face of the world's corrupt experience. Allworthy, for example, despite his preaching of prudence, is relatively innocent when one considers the variety of selfish villains with whom he has surrounded himself, and who impose on him. Squire Western is relatively innocent too, like some of Robinson Crusoe's savages: he has no control over any of his passions, and no conception of anyone's living by any code other than his. The Man of the Hill, as Tom says, is embittered because he had been hurt when he was innocent and inexperienced, and he therefore is blindly misanthropic, like the similarly distorted Gulliver at the end of Swift's work. Though they evidence all the raw qualities of man, both of good and of bad, the country people in the novel are unprepared for the complex experience of London. Through the great wealth and power of Allworthy, the fortunate discovery of Tom's birth, the intense goodness of Sophia, and the incompetence of the villains, innocence is enlightened with a minimum of corruption. But its triumph is a near thing.

By the time of *Amelia,* Fielding's sympathy with innocence was mixed with impatience at the folly and pride with which it can meet the world. Amelia alone among the innocents escapes censure, because Fielding makes her so prudent that she can intuitively conquer experience, like Richardson's Clarissa. She understands the aims of the lord and Colonel James in good time and arranges her defenses accordingly. Booth is inexperienced enough to be fooled by a variety of swindlers, beginning with the Methodist pickpocket and Robinson and going on to Captain Trent, the lying influence peddler, and the rest. For such impositions, Fielding pities him. But the interlude with Miss Matthews suggests an irresponsibility which had been lacking in the more widely promiscuous Tom and which may well underlie the Booths' further troubles. Mrs. Bennet also had been insufficiently alert to danger when she, her husband, and her little boy came to London, and she had allowed herself to be lured to the catastrophic masquerade by a free ticket: "Innocence, it is true, possessed my heart; but it was innocence unguarded, intoxicated with foolish desires, and liable to every temptation" (VII, vii). Where the earlier works are set largely in fantasies and concerned largely with ideal innocence as one moral goal, in *Amelia* the social consequences of unguarded innocence are so bad as to make it culpable. Its misunderstanding of the world—in Booth and Mrs. Bennet, and perhaps even in Dr. Harrison—has something of the wilfully delusive and self-destructive about it. A mind which must act in the world yet refuses to see the world as clearly as possible is prideful and irresponsible, no matter how well disposed in other respects.

A major symbol of Fielding's ambiguous view of excursive innocence is Don Quixote, who fascinated him throughout his career. The deluded knight becomes a superb image of the man who is enclosed within his vision of the world, and for that reason is mad, sometimes ludicrously mad; but his vision is often morally superior to the actuality of the world, and for that reason his nature is admirable. He cannot make his vision prevail over marred circumstances—all the virtuous figures from the country cannot make of the city the ideal commonwealth that Plato causes them to expect—but the attempt, while often laughable, is praiseworthy.

Aside from the absurdity of Adams, Fielding's other ambivalent references to quixotism show that however he admires a mind virtuously insulated against the world, he nonetheless sees it as ridiculous and self-defeating in its refusal or inability to understand how to cope with actuality. He regularly lectured his good-natured figures on the need to learn—artificially, against their "natures"—how other minds work and how social and economic forces affect character. His "Essay on Conversation" is such a lecture, for which his fiction can be seen as illustrative slides, whose intent is to educate such minds to the nature of the world around them. Holy idiots, men who are good without the qualifications of greatness, seem to Fielding almost babies, and babies cannot act effectively. These virtuous people have managed to bypass the outer sphere of action on the road to inward contentment; their contentment may therefore be illusory.[9]

A frequent image which Fielding associates with quixotism is the enchanted castle, the place in which all sorts of strange and embarrassing things happen to a principal character, in which apparently fixed relationships suddenly take on new form. In *Love in Several Masques,* for example, a darkened drawing room becomes a scene of complete confusion and mistaken identity for several characters: at times they feel that they are being deceived by magic, and yet their relationships are much clarified as a result of it. Similarly, in *The Temple Beau* confusions and revelations in the beau's chambers suggest that Fielding has found the device of untying the knot much facilitated by mistaken identities within a strange room. The same purpose is served by a bedroom in *The Letter Writers* and a back room at an inn in *The Coffee-House Politician.* In *Don Quixote in England,* the hero frequently comments on the innkeeper's being the governor of a castle and an evil enchanter; as in the other plays, the plot entanglements are most confused and magically unraveled in this castle. Here are almost formal preparations for Lady Booby's mansion, Tom's inn at Upton, and Booth's Newgate. Similarly, the device of bringing the characters to masquerades is an aspect of the reality-illusion theme, of which innocence-experience is another aspect and quixotism is the central image.

In the family relationships in the novels, certain patterns recur which seem to reflect archetypal fantasies deriving from childhood. Often these patterns involve family divisions among siblings, and often misunderstandings between children and parents. *Joseph Andrews* has less of this sort of subject than the other novels, since most of the characters have no parents or siblings to speak of until the denouement. And since the subject at the beginning is the burlesque of *Pamela,* we are required to have Joseph writing to his family with the canting sweetness that revolted Fielding in Richardson's book. Still, at one of the crises in the unknotting of the various parentages, the incest theme appears, as it does importantly in *Tom ·Jones.* The burlesque unraveling of the knot reminds Fielding of another confused case of identity: the senior Andrews' were "kindly received by the Lady Booby, whose heart went now pit-a-pat, as did those of Joseph and Fanny. They felt perhaps little less anxiety in this interval than Oedipus himself, whilst his fate was revealing" (IV, xv). No doubt the relations between Joseph and Lady Booby, like the many other situations in Fielding's plays and novels involving young men and considerably older women,[10] in some way reflect an interest in Oedipus' difficulties, but whether the cause is Fielding's psychology or his intimate knowledge of French farce and Restoration comedy, I cannot say.

In *Tom Jones,* Sophia has learned to manage her father in normal times: she mollifies his violence by playing his favorite songs for his drunken pleasure, showing directly how children's fantasies of the size and danger of parents connect with folklore and fairy tale. The interactions of Squire Western and his sister, and of both with Sophia, seem also reflections of this process; indeed, *Tom Jones* is full of elders who act like ogres toward the young, particularly on the issue of marriage. Perhaps of all the archetypal substance which Fielding uses as the base of comic plotting this is the most primitive, the most charged with ambiguous emotions, and the most effective in direct communication with the reader, as the immense success of Richardson's *Clarissa* showed. The story of the Man of the Hill indicates the arbitrariness of this myth: it assumes as given, as a premise, that his mother preferred his brother and hated him—no reasons are assigned for this apparently peculiar behavior, except that the father preferred the narrator.

Tom Jones finds himself in a situation which combines a good many of the story patterns of romance and fairy tale with issues which are recognizably the psychological projections of childhood. While the early opposition of Blifil and Tom is the basis for the major thematic contrast of cold prudence with impulsive goodness, it is a clear pattern of sibling rivalry, an archetype going back to Cain and Abel. An immense lineup of villains tries to destroy Tom, particularly Square, Thwackum (whose description often suggests gigantism), and Blifil. They are fought by All-worthy (the father who does his best to judge but often acts incomprehensibly toward the son), Western (the lunatic extreme of an arbitrary father-God), and Sophia, the alma mater. After Tom has performed the tasks and undergone the sufferings which purify and mature him, he is reconciled to Allworthy and Western. The villains, so dangerous in youth, have been rendered powerless, and Tom is the "happiest of all humankind" with his Sophia. Like life in the Wilson household as described by Adams (a household which Joseph's emulated after the reunion with his own all-wise father) and like the life of the Booths at the end of *Amelia*, "this was the manner in which the people had lived in the Golden Age" (*JA*, III, iv). Despite Fielding's many examples to the contrary, he always—in the essays, plays, and novels—argued that the high point of happiness lay within the circle of the virtuous family, as he argued that it existed within the circle of the virtuous mind.

The plot elements in various autobiographical narratives in the last novel are marked by even more severe family strains. Miss Matthews' seducer ran off, but "Indeed his fear of my brother was utterly groundless, for I believe he would rather have thanked any man who had destroyed me; and I am sure I am not in the least behindhand with him in good wishes" (I, ix). Amelia's own mother —we hear nothing of her father, from whom she presumably inherited her mind and gentle nature—was a witch-like "woman of violent passions." Though Booth, atypically in Fielding, had loved his sister (who is, however, dead), Amelia's sister Betty is vicious, as we might expect.

Some of these familial patterns are notable as persisting through successive novels. Mrs. Bennet's early problems with her passionate father and her passionate aunt, for example, are variations of Sophia's. In the Booth-Harrison confusions, also, Fielding provides a condensed version of the Tom-Allworthy ones, in which appearances are much against the son and at times cause the well-disposed father to be extremely severe. Both Tom and Booth, like Wilson before them, suffer when the guidance of a wise, fatherly figure is temporarily removed. In general, while Fielding is not so sensitive to the details of psychological friction within the family as is Richardson, he everywhere reflects an awareness of its larger forms which is perhaps more responsible. Nowhere are the relations between parents and children in his novels so idyllically simplified as those of Pamela and the older Andrews; nowhere does he show sisters so adoring or a brother so responsibly adorable as the Grandisons. To follow one of the threads of a wooly term, if Fielding is sentimental in some of his techniques, he is never sentimental when family relationships are his subject.

This is not to say that nothing in the family can be good. When the filial relationship works properly, Fielding finds it most admirable of all. Adams is a father to his flock, which follows him faithfully; Allworthy, Harrison, and the gypsy king are everyone's father. Since they are all sincere in fulfilling the paternal role—which Fielding sees almost exclusively in terms of guidance and protection—they are all beloved by their symbolic children.

Connected with this relationship is the idea of the paternal ruler. The gypsy leader is closest to the Bolingbroke model, a true patriot king, who does nothing except for the good of his people and is consequently treated by them with dutiful and loving respect. Allworthy, more generalized, provides the model of fatherly rule, for he is concerned only with the welfare of those in his family and his jurisdiction; but his frequent susceptibility to trickery illustrates a central deficiency in all monarchic ideals. An ideal, which is essentially a self-enclosed theory, cannot work in the outer world. Immediately after describing the gypsy establishment, Fielding develops an elaborate essay against the idea of the patriot king, on the ground that the actual world has always been lacking in men able to limit their own desires when their power is unlimited.

The value of paternal rule seems to depend on the distance to which people can send outgoing feelings. Some leaders, like Wild, are completely self-enclosed, and repudiate all responsibility for anyone else's welfare. Most people, however, care enough for their children to yield to their needs, though *Tom Jones* is full of fathers, like the Quaker, or Western, or the older Nightingale, who refuse to consider their children as individuals distinct from themselves. Relatively few men have paternal responsibilities far beyond their immediate families, and even among noblemen, country squires, and priests, those well enough disposed to fulfil them, like Adams, Harrison, and Allworthy, are rare and fallible. It is

obvious to Fielding, then, that the combination of a sufficient
of virtuous effluence with the immense and complex expe
necessary for the proper rule of a nation is so rare in one that .
to be miraculous. Consequently, only a limited monarchy will do.
Failing that, the best arrangement may be the one in effect where
Mrs. Heartfree is shipwrecked: the ruler has much power, but besides undergoing daily lessons in humility, he is annually examined for the justice of his behavior and subject to deposition if
he has performed unsatisfactorily. The ideal father-king is able to
go out of himself, to deny his own pleasures for the good of his
children-subjects, to make the serene order of his mind the pattern for order among the combating siblings of the commonwealth. Besides acting well, he also has the very high function of
teaching his children moral action and the nature of reality, of
preparing them in turn and in their spheres to be fathers and
rulers. But through ignorance of the world (Adams) he may be an
insufficient teacher, and through confusion between his role and
his nature he may become proud, hence self-enclosed, hence useless or vicious in performing his function.

Another of Fielding's favorite archetypes, the country idyl with
which the virtuous are rewarded, has been frequently discussed by
recent critics. In his two important essays on Fielding, George
Sherburn most clearly indicated the country-town contrast in the
novels, a contrast which is fundamental to the innocence-experience pattern and to the pattern of virtue sallying out of its refuge
within the mind to act charitably in the world. In his "Fielding's
Amelia," Sherburn says, "Fielding drops his high spirits whenever he writes about London. Even in *Tom Jones* the London
episodes are all somber, and Lady Bellaston and Lord Fellamar
belong as much to the atmosphere of *Amelia* as they do to that of
Tom Jones" (p. 148). In "Fielding's Social Outlook," Sherburn
says, "whenever he writes about London his tone becomes grim,
hard, distressing" (p. 10). Maynard Mack carries this perception a
step further, making the country and city the chief structural elements in the first novel: "The two poles of value in *Joseph Andrews* (as later in *Tom Jones*) are the country-world and the city,
neither perfect, but the former superior to the latter because more
honest. In the first book the relative honesty of the country pene-
trates to the city in the person of Joseph and, having resisted corruption there, is reinforced in its withdrawal by another of its

representatives, Adams. In the last book the relative hypocrisy of the city-world (Lady Booby, Beau Didapper, and the rest) invades the country and is again defeated, the action alternating back and forth between country and city symbols. . . ."[11] Lady Booby's house thus becomes a city symbol and Adams' a country one, and these contrasting poles also are shown in the stories of Leonora and Mr. Wilson. There are weaknesses in this analysis, particularly toward the end (why should Lady Booby's manor, a fundamental part of the country economy and social structure,[12] be exclusively symbolic of the city?), but it is valid in the main.

Though the tenor of the general discussions of Fielding's use of the country-city contrast is accurate, the actual evidence from Fielding's writings is not so uniform as some critics suggest.[13] (And it must be recalled that Fielding spent his adult life in the city, with very short excursions to his favorite countryside, though he would not have found it impossible to support himself outside of London.) In general, Fielding brings all his major figures to London because that is the major scene for human action, just as the mind must work outwardly because there is nowhere else to do good or evil. After they have found the arena bewildering and dangerous but have demonstrated the necessary willingness to act virtuously, he returns them to their country retirements, as the consequences of right action return to the mind to dispense tranquility there. He is under no delusions about the imperfections of the country or about its stultifying effects upon the uneducated or lazy; he is only sure that under the right circumstances of wealth, family, and internal satisfaction it *can* permit serene retirement, whereas the city provides constant, perhaps even insurmountable, challenges to integrity.

Though Fielding's aim is always to reveal the world in which we must act, his method is not consistently realistic. Rather, he shows us in his novels the parallels and contrasts provided by the enclosed world on the one hand—the world of gentle or violent delusions, the world of pattern and order, the world of wish fulfilment, the world of the ideal—and the world of eighteenth-century actuality on the other. One kind of delusive world, he suggests, is factitious: that in which selfish fantasies, such as Peter Pounce's or Lady Bellaston's, provide enclosure against reality or that in which romancers or other lying writers attempt to disguise actuality by performing miracles of character transformation. To have any meaning, the actions must occur in the actual and dangerous world. Adams and Joseph and Tom sally out among ruffians, hypocrites, lechers, and brutes, but they pursue virtue nonetheless; and while Booth is not so steadfast, his will is good. The fantasy for Fielding lies in the reward for this action, in plot and not in character; his miracles involve revelations, not conversions. As the mind returns to the rewards of serenity after working outward to do good, so his heroes, having demonstrated courageous good will in the dangerous and complex world, earn their serene reward in the country.

In developing his juxtaposed reality (which is incoherent outside though coherent within the minds of the virtuous) and fantasy (the projection outward of the mind's wishes) Fielding uses as his base certain archetypes of human life, the most notable being the confrontation of experience by the innocent. His innocents, preserved from within, are themselves largely protected from pollution, though a narrative like the autobiography of the Man of the Hill reminds us of the grave possibility of that despair which is to the moralist the ultimate defeat. The innocent heroes, like Tom or Booth, become involved in shady actions, but their dispositions are not hurt. Booth's intellect is slightly corrupted by his misfortunes, in that he accepts Mandevillian determinism; but this external blemish is easily removed by reading Barrow and listening to Harrison, both of whom speak directly to Booth's good disposition.

At times, the achievement of experience is in terms of primordial fantasies, such as those involving the child's dealing with a world of elderly ogres. The older women who assault the passions, and sometimes the bodies, of the heroes are of the same stuff as the witches of child lore; the violently aggressive adult males, from the mad squire of *Joseph Andrews,* through Jonathan Wild and Northerton, to the lord in *Amelia,* are again grotesques of adults in the child's fantasy. Of the heroes, only Adams—who is significantly described as a child in the ways of the world—and Tom are sturdy enough knights errant to dispose of the arbitrary ogres. Tom even copes with the exaggerated Thwackum as a true child hero should: after Tom's only early example of pure sexuality, he buffets Thwackum most satisfyingly. Whatever more complex psychological explanation might be sought, it is clear that at least the exaggerated power of older people is an extension of the fantasies of childhood. Indeed, the exaggerated evil of siblings of the heroes or heroines may, again, be the consequence of seeing the family from the viewpoint of children—as in current novels, we have the subjective fantasies derived from sibling rivalry. Similarly, the view of authority may well reflect the child's response to paternal benevolence and arbitrariness.

Like all useful miracles, those in the plots of the novels—from the last-minute rescues and the revelation of Joseph's and Fanny's births, through Mrs. Heartfree's escapes, Tom's extrication from his horrors, and the discovery of the forging of Amelia's mother's will—indicate by contrast the normal state of the world. It is a largely grim and decayed world, in which goodness can expect none but an internal reward. Unlike classical comedy, Fielding's does not assert the values of society as a positive counter to the oddity of the comic figures. He does affirm the traditional ideal of society; but he is uniformitarian enough to believe that the ideals have never been approximated, that society has always been dangerous for the good, that fantasies in literature and the self-approving joy of the mind have been the only guarantors of happiness. Don Quixote's Spain and Alceste's France were on the whole tolerable societies to their authors, however inferior to the comic figures' visions. Ben Jonson's worlds are predatory, but his characters are no more admirable than their contexts, with the implied ideals—the reasonable, controlled men of good will—also implied victors in any contest with society. To Fielding, however, as in the picaresque tradition, virtue is no shield, and even reason (as witness Allworthy) no certain help. With Swift, Pope, Richardson, and Smollett, he shares the central fear of eighteenth-century literature, a vision of a disintegrating world under the sway of chaos and old night.

VII

Conclusion

GRANTED THAT a sense of man's inevitable isolation within himself is pervasive in the eighteenth century, as witness *A Tale of a Tub,* Gray's poems, *Rasselas,* and the supreme example, *Tristram Shandy;* granted also that "sympathy," the ability to leave the self and perceive the nature of another, is a conventional ideal in the mid-eighteenth century, and that holding both these views involved a good many writers in an inevitable contradiction; still, in no other writer of the time is this conflict so evident or so central as in Fielding. To Fielding, man's basic duty was the need to understand and sympathize with others, and his basic problem was psychological isolation.

This view of the human paradox manifests itself everywhere in Fielding's writings, in his psychology, moral philosophy, social attitudes, themes, and techniques. In no one else except Sterne is misunderstanding—the inability to communicate because of mental preoccupations, social restrictions, delusions of all sorts—so recurrent and fundamental a comic device. Even Fielding's chief overt theme, the distinction between appearance and reality, reflects the central paradox of moral epistemology. If man is self-enclosed by his passions, with reason primarily an agent for conveying enough reality to prevent self-destruction, then everyone must face the problem of finding his way past vanity—his tendency to delude himself, as well as the tendency of others to fool themselves—and hypocrisy, the attempt of others to appear what they are not.

Of the two the illusion fostered by society at the expense of the individual is more amenable to comic portrayal. Vanity, which is properly the subject of a comic-pathetic combination, most conspicuously in *Don Quixote,* is less frequent as an influence on Fielding's heroes than hypocrisy. That is, his sympathetic figures are unlikely to be deluding themselves to provide fun for us. Adams, who comes closest to this, is not at all mistaken about the values in which he believes, values which Fielding urges, though he sometimes laughs at their impracticality. Rather, his major characters are shown being educated, and the medium of education is the exposure of the falseness of much of the society around them. In this view, Fielding's great gift is not the perception of man's essential nature through the complexities of individual characters, but an ability to present man's condition in society, in which the ironies of existence are shown through what happens to people and what might happen to them. What they feel is likely to be the expression of Fielding's theories of general psychology and morality as they cope with his vision of eighteenth-century reality.

In Fielding's view, man is inevitably limited by the nature of his mind, determined on the whole by the cast of his disposition—whether indrawn or outgoing, whether Mandeville's or Shaftesbury's model. Man is subjected to passions, and he is therefore a prey to delusions and to the imposition of hypocrisy as he tries to deal with the outside actuality. As an aid in assessing reality (but not in determining disposition) he may have reason and its experiential subsidiary, prudence. The good disposition needs religion as well to confirm, to embolden, and to direct it; and the overwhelming need is to be aware of the humanity of others, so that we may understand them, respond to them, and act suitably on the dictates of our charitable impulses. For Fielding as for Sterne man needs to go out of himself—virtue demands good works—but his rewards come from within. The knowledge of having done virtuously leads to mental peace, Fielding's highest good, as the response to wrong action is internal distress. Since his range among people and actions is much wider than Sterne's, he is faced with far more complex decisions on practical morality and practical psychology.

A great question throughout Fielding's career is whether delusive happiness, the production of credulous and innocent good nature, is better than experience. On the whole, he thinks it is not, except for the wealthy and good country squire, since it is too unstable, too subject to distortion. Good nature is the essential requisite for a good character, but it is not enough. By the late works, *Amelia* and the *Journal,* Fielding is convinced that in addition to the guard of reason and the spur of religion good nature needs a sufficient stock of experience so that it may act responsibly. Man must act in society, because it is the proper arena for the good disposition and because there is nowhere else to act. He must therefore be capable of defending himself against the distortions by which the selfishness of others, whether as individuals or in professional or social groups, attempts to exploit the innocent. He must learn to see more than the reflections of his own well-disposed mind.

The social context offers a larger avenue for action, and therefore a larger opportunity for the display of virtue, than the limited enclosure of the small family. For the family, the relatively passive virtue of women is ideally suited. For virtue in society, the best candidate is the man fortified by courage, religion, experience, and position. Though in theory the ruler of a nation has the widest scope of all, the temptations to the pride which we all have and the impediments in the way of clear understanding are so great that it is almost impossible to find ideal rulers, except of such limited establishments as the gypsy monarchy. Even the high political nobility is so corrupted by the pressures of wealth and party that examples in it are rare. It is possible, however, to find a kind of golden mean of situation, as with the powerful country squires like Allworthy.

To satisfy oneself, and to have the widest opportunity to act well in the world, one must preserve a good reputation, where that is consistent with vigorous action. A man's standing within the few miles that form the circumference of his world (to borrow Sterne's image) can decide whether he will be allowed to act virtuously. He will need to conform to some of the world's arrangements, essentially the arrangements provided by the larger society for the sake of convenient social living: conventions, like the rules of good breeding and the division into classes, which ideally guarantee consideration of the human rights of others, but which can be and have been easily turned into tools for confusing and dehumanizing others.

But not only the formal social order or the rules of good breeding may become poisonous instruments. One of the sadder impediments in Fielding's plan to educate ignorant virtue to the nature of the world (his motive, both stated and implicit, from the *Miscellanies* to the *Journal*) is the distortion, introduced by selfishness, of all words used to describe ideal conditions or actions. Indeed, this distrust of words seems to have been part of Fielding's motive for writing narrative fiction as against essays: "an example is a kind of picture, in which virtue becomes, as it were, an object of sight and strikes us with an idea of that loveliness, which Plato asserts there is in her naked charms" (dedication to *Tom Jones*). If we are disposed toward virtue, then an able novel can cause our sympathetic imagination to experience Tom's moral choices, as no verbal exhortation addressed to our reason could.

This suspicion of words, supported by Lockean epistemology,[1] is one of the reasons why Fielding plays with the idea of prudence, as well as with the other qualities which may be good but have been trivialized and formalized by selfishness acting in society. Such qualities, which are necessary to describe, support, and direct the good disposition, become counters for the ill-disposed in their operations in the corrupt world of appearances. Prudence becomes a mask for cold selfish withdrawal or manipulation, as with Peter Pounce or Blifil or Mrs. Ellison; love, a delusive or hypocritical name for lust or hunger in Lady Booby or Lady Bellaston or Colonel James or the unnamed lord; reason, as with various stoics and occasional shocked innocents, an excuse for withdrawal and despair; religion, an instrument for the selfish repression of others, as with Thwackum or Trulliber; reputation, a cloak for hypocrisy, not a reward for virtue; law, a mechanism for exploitation; and charity, the most glorious ideal of all, merely a word invoked by selfishness. There is no cure for these crimes against sympathetic communication except experience enlightened, if possible, by the direction of an older person who is capable of supporting the ideals attached to these words while indicating their frequent corruption. Without such direction, as the Man of the Hill shows, the discovery of society's allegiance to words alone, of the ways in which our routine lives are an infernal parody of the good life, may lead to a despair in man which prevents our acting for the good. We may be satisfied with formalized, mediocre qualities instead of the ideals, and therefore live a false version of the intense joys of human communication.

Fielding's insistence on the need for faith in man leads inevitably to the question of whether, and to what degree, he was "sentimental." Various recent scholars unite in describing the prevailing trend in the middle and late eighteenth century as sentimental but agree on few if any of its criteria. The word has been used to describe certain kindly assumptions about human nature; an unwillingness to face the existence of evil in man or in society; a wish to exalt the bourgeoisie and its addiction to mediocrity and compromise; a tortuous insistence on happy endings, preferably after agonizing plots; and a reliance on easy devices for eliciting the reader's or audience's emotional involvement.[2] Not surprisingly, Fielding is a sentimentalist by some of these criteria and something else—perhaps a curmudgeon—by others.

If sentimentalism consists in faith in communication primarily through feeling rather than through the intellectual apprehension of words—a confluence of Locke and the latitudinarians—then Fielding is a sentimentalist. Probably he holds no other idea so strongly as the central importance of sympathetic communication in both epistemology and morality. Those evil people who cannot sympathize with goodness do not understand it intellectually either; they simply feel that the good are knaves like themselves or fools incapable of the intelligence of knaves. In short, they cannot at all communicate if they cannot sympathize, except that for a time at least they can simulate virtue so far as its external signs have been provided for them through the forms of society. As a corollary, Fielding can use the techniques of sentimentalism —frequent kneelings, apostrophes to heaven, violently emotional scenes, hairbreadth escapes treated seriously, visions of a mother prattling to her children—when his prime intention, as in *Amelia*, is to open the hearts of his readers. But in earlier works such devices are rare and often ironic, perhaps because he relies on his readers to apprehend the more subtle morality of comedy.

If benevolism—the doctrine that the moral aim of man should be doing good among his fellows—is central to sentimentalism, then here again Fielding is guilty; though whether a criterion which would also admit Swift and Joyce and Sartre to the school is valid, I rather doubt. The assumption that happiness is compatible with virtue on this earth would also be a sentimental touchstone that admits Fielding; worse yet, he sentimentally makes happiness the supreme goal of human life. But it must be added, and this may cancel his admission, that except for a few favored country squires the compatibility is to be only in the mind—an argument essentially Platonic and Christian. Last in the damning array, he tends to imply that the sins of good nature, such as promiscuous sexuality, carelessness, dangerous gullibility, may be forgivable.[3] But he hedges this tolerance with the argument that habituation to such sins corrupts, that they tend to be annexed to other and worse qualities, and that society is likely to hurt their possessors even when they are well intentioned. Sexual excess he seems to tolerate in Betty the chambermaid, in Tom Jones, and even in Booth; but in all cases the sinners are drastically punished, and the dangers to their natures if they persist are made very clear. Furthermore, as he grew older he found it harder and harder to forgive gullibility, since it was likely to entail the major sin of irresponsibility: he is careful to make Booth pay in mental distress for the effect of his follies on his family.

On the basis of other criteria, Fielding turns out not to be a sentimentalist at all. He does not, for example, assume that virtue triumphs; though in his comedies and even in *Amelia* he arranges to have happy endings, he makes it abundantly clear that not society but the good mind is the source of happiness. More fundamentally, he is not enough of a Shaftesburian to assume that all people are basically good, though he does say that most are potentially so. He makes no apology for the evil of Blifil or Lady Bellaston or Amelia's lord; some people are that way, and they must be restrained, as dangerous criminals must be executed. Furthermore, he does not think that character can suddenly or easily change for the better (as with Mr. B. in *Pamela*, whom he twice ridiculed). The reforms at the end of *Tom Jones* are only of the good-natured, and that of Robinson in *Amelia* ends in a halter.

To the sentimental exaltation of the middle classes Fielding does not subscribe. His criteria for virtue are relatively austere and uncompromising; whatever bourgeois characters or activities he shows are almost uniformly objectionable. Wilson's competitors in the wine trade, presumably ordinary businessmen, were all adulterators among whom no honest man could thrive; lawyer Dowling makes the compromises necessary to allow for a successful practice, and if these are not sufficiently damning, Fielding has him join in an attempt on Tom's freedom. Indeed, all professions —so much admired by the middle classes—and trades are equally damned insofar as they impose selfish concerns on their practitioners. Again, the modified view of sentimentalism which Krutch has attributed to Richardson in *Clarissa,* the assumption that anyone typically good can be considered tragic, is not shared by Fielding. He is too much of a classical scholar to make the Booth family tragic, and actually emphasizes again and again their relative smallness; they are vastly pathetic, and capable of being even more pathetic, but he avoids imputing greatness to them. In short, while Fielding completely subscribed to the humanitarianism which was more and more characteristic of English thought in the period, he had far too strong a sense of the existence of evil and of the dangers of society to be a moral or philosophical sentimentalist; too great an abhorrence of the commercial ethic to make the bourgeoisie admirable; and too much respect for learning, tradition, and literary decorum to tamper with his art in the interests of the maudlin and the saccharine.

In his various estimations of the function of the writer, Fielding again praises a heightened ability for sympathetic communication as well as a roving out to perform good offices. The issue is moral, as it is in the *Essay on Criticism;* but it is also psychological. Bad writers imagine from their own disordered brains. Romance writers, Fielding argues in *Tom Jones,* reproduce in their incoherent and painful works the incoherent and painful chimeras of their generally bad minds (IV, i). In such passages, he is saying of romancers what Swift had advanced against modern hacks in both the *Battle of the Books* and the *Tale of a Tub,* that they are sickly limited to their own minds rather than able to range like the bee over all of humanity. Good and useful writers are able to direct their minds outward, perceive the world around them, and reorder in their art what they have understood. They provide well observed and recorded human character, which is eternally recurrent and eternally true.[4] The good novel is the perfect interaction of the roving mind of the novelist and the reality around him, recorded meaningfully in the serene world of art. The work of art, well-ordered like *Tom Jones,* is the happy work, a parallel to the well-ordered mind.

It is therefore natural that Fielding considers the highest faculty of the artist to be the ability to range out among mankind for the food of his art, just as the well-disposed mind ranges out for the food of its virtue. In his definition of invention in *Tom Jones* he makes this point explicitly: invention is not, he says, "a creative faculty," the sort of thing which characterizes bad romances.[5] By creative faculty he evidently means what Swift meant in his image of the spider working from its own bowels. Coleridge's definition of the creative imagination as an imitation of God's creativity would simply have seemed to Fielding the high point of modern hubris. Rather, invention is "discovery, or finding out . . . a quick and sagacious penetration into the true essence of all the objects of our contemplation" (IX, i). When he speaks of the novelist's need to have "conversation," he is concerned with the diversity of human nature which is to be discovered and exhibited only by the personality which has ranged far outside itself. Later in *Tom Jones,* he calls Genius to his aid, again for the purpose of providing the information for the roving novelist: "Teach me, which to thee is no difficult task, to know mankind better than they know themselves. Remove that mist which dims the intellects of mortals, and causes them to adore men for their art, or to detest them for their cunning, in deceiving others, when they are, in reality, the objects only of ridicule, for deceiving themselves" (XIII, i). Next, he asks the aid of Humanity, "almost the constant attendant on true genius": knowing the essences in a good mind— and only a good mind can know them—inevitably entails human sympathy. Third, he seeks Learning, which is to act like the reason, to shape and evaluate the products of genius and the feelings of humanity; and last, Experience: "From thee only can the manners of mankind be known; to which the recluse pedant, however great his parts or extensive his learning may be, hath ever been a stranger" (XIII, i).

Genius is, then, the faculty which helps to discover the essences of human nature; experience is the data derived from contact with the material into which Genius is to rove. With the aid of experience, humanity, and learning, genius can fetch truths, and from them form the true novel.[6] Human nature is the field for the novelist's action, from which he is to cull the materials for his work;[7] the imagination, by contrast, is the product of enclosed and conflicting passions, and it therefore cannot provide the truth which is the province of art. As the implications of this view became clearer for Fielding and as he became even more committed to reality as his subject, he set off in directions that were unusual in his period and immediately after.

The older Fielding finds the ancients dangerously imaginative, in contrast to the widespread admiration of them which generally characterized the eighteenth century. In the *Journal,* which has as its aim truth rather narrowly interpreted, Fielding says that the ancient poets "found the limits of nature too strait for the immensity of their genius, which they had not room to exert, without extending fact by fiction" (p. 26). These ancients, he complains, turn "fiction into reality. Their paintings are so bold, their colours so strong, that every thing they touch seems to exist in the very manner they represent it: their portraits are so just, and their landscapes so beautiful, that we acknowledge the strokes of nature in both, without enquiring whether nature herself, or her journeyman the poet, formed the first pattern of the piece" (p. 26). Even in landscape they imposed their brilliant imaginations upon their readers; the cliffs of Dover, for example, owe all their fame to the somewhat less ancient Shakespeare: "In truth, mountains, rivers, heroes and gods owe great part of their existence to the poets; and Greece and Italy do so plentifully abound in the former, because they furnished so glorious a number of the latter" (p. 67). Therefore their trivial streams and hillocks are celebrated, while much nobler ones elsewhere are unknown. Therefore also, such authors, no matter how great, have followed self-pleasing fancy and irresponsibly misinformed mankind about reality.

Such a view is too extreme a denial of the creative faculty in art, and we are not surprised that its proponent should have produced the irritably prosaic *Amelia.* But that one stage in the road to this dead end can be an almost perfect reconciliation of the mind of the artist, the world in which we live, and the claims of society (in the person of the reader) we can see in *Tom Jones.* Arguments over how much moral concern can dance on the point of a well-shaped novel are as inconclusive as their medieval predecessors. But whatever the approach, one cannot deny to Fielding the achievement of uniting serenity with truth, of celebrating life in an ordered repudiation of that orderliness which is death, matched in the English novel only by Jane Austen, James Joyce, and Joseph Conrad.

Notes

I. *The Enclosed Self*

1. John Locke, *Essay Concerning Human Understanding,* in *Works* (Germany: Scientia Verlag Aalen, 1963; a rpt. of London, 1823), Bk. II, Chap. i, Sec. 3. Subsequent references to the *Essay* will be to this edition and will cite book, chapter, and section. On Locke's pervasive influence in the century, see Kenneth MacLean, *John Locke and English Literature of the Eighteenth Century* (New York: Russell and Russell, 1962; a rpt. of New Haven: Yale University Press, 1936). Mr. MacLean opens his preface with the bald statement, which his book proves, that "The book that had most influence in the Eighteenth Century, the Bible excepted, was Locke's Essay Concerning Human Understanding (1690)."

2. John Traugott, in his *Tristram Shandy's World* (Berkeley & Los Angeles: University of California Press, 1954), p. 10, summarizes the epistemological problem that Locke presents: for Locke the mind is substance, substance is unknowable, and therefore every mind lives isolated: "Consequently the effects of mental substance, ideas, and affections as perceived can be communicated only by the happy circumstance that minds may be caused to think alike by an exactly determined language." See also Arthur H. Cash, "The Lockean Psychology of *Tristram Shandy,*" *ELH,* XXII (1955), 125-35; Ernest Lee Tuveson, *The Imagination as a Means of Grace* (Berkeley & Los Angeles: University of California Press, 1960), *passim,* esp. pp. 18-25.

3. The most effective and extensive presentation of Fielding's indebtedness to the latitudinarian divines has been Martin C. Battestin's *The Moral Basis of Fielding's Art* (Middletown: Wesleyan University Press, 1959). Henry Knight Miller, in his encyclopedic *Essays on Fielding's Miscellanies* (Princeton: Princeton University Press, 1961), pp. 65 ff., tends to place the influence of the benevolist divines lower than that of the classical moralists like Cicero, but he does not deny that influence. See also William Robert Irwin, *The Making of Jonathan Wild* (New York: Columbia University Press, 1941); James A. Work, "Henry Fielding, Christian Censor," in *The Age of Johnson,* ed. Frederick W. Hilles (New Haven: Yale University Press, 1949), pp. 139-48; A. R. Towers, "Fielding and Dr. Samuel Clarke," *MLN,* LXX (1955), 257-60; Ralph W. Rader, "Ralph Cudworth and Fielding's *Amelia,*" *MLN,* LXXI (1956), 336-8; D. S. Thomas, "Fortune and the Passions in Fielding's *Amelia,*" *MLR,* LX (1965), 176-87.

4. R. S. Crane, "Suggestions Toward a Genealogy of the 'Man of Feeling,'" *ELH,* I (1934), 217.

5. Bernard Mandeville, *The Fable of the Bees: or, Private Vices, Publick Benefits,* ed. F. B. Kaye (Oxford: Clarendon Press, 1924), I, 80. For a discus-

sion of Mandeville's effect on Fielding, see Le Roy W. Smith, "Fielding and Mandeville: The 'War Against Virtue,' " *Criticism*, III (1961), 7-15.

6. ". . . in a sensible Creature, That which is not done thro any Affection at all, makes neither Good nor Ill in the nature of that Creature; who then only is supos'd Good, when the Good or Ill of the System to which he has relation, is the immediate Object of some Passion or Affection moving him": *Characteristicks of Men, Women, Opinions, Times*, 6th ed. (London, 1737), II, 21; "We have found, that to deserve the name of *Good* or *Virtuous*, a Creature must have all his Inclinations and Affections, his Dispositions of Mind and Temper, sutable, and agreeing with the Good of his *Kind*, or of that *System* in which he is included, and of which he constitutes a PART. To stand thus well affected, and to have one's Affections *right* and *intire*, not only in respect of one's self, but of Society and the Publick: This is *Rectitude, Integrity*, or VIRTUE" (II, 77).

7. As Cecil A. Moore pointed out early, "Instead of the sordid utilitarianism of the orthodox, Shaftesbury proposed as the only reward of virtuous conduct the immediate satisfaction it produces, which is the only genuine happiness to be attained by man": "Shaftesbury and the Ethical Poets in England, 1700-1760," *PMLA*, XXI (1916), 269.

8. *Moral Basis of Fielding's Art*, p. 84.

9. Fielding's view that disdain, a conscious disregard for the humanity of others, was one of the worst possible elements in human nature did not change, as witness the following from a *Covent-Garden Journal* paper of August 29, 1752: "THERE is not in Human Nature a more odious Disposition, than a Proneness to Contempt. Nor is there any which more certainly denotes a bad Mind. For in a good, and benign Temper, there can be no Room for this Sensation. That which constitutes an Object of Contempt to the Malevolent, becomes the Object of other Passions to a worthy and good-natur'd Man: For in such a Person, Wickedness and Vice, must raise Hatred and Abhorrence; and Weakness and Folly will be sure to excite Compassion; so that he will find no Object of his Contempt, in all the Actions of Men" *(CGJ*, II, 88-89).

10. The world's susceptibility to imposition by false reputations, so important in both *Tom Jones* and *Amelia*, is foreshadowed in *The Temple Beau* (1730), in which Veromil says that his brother probably maligned him while he was abroad: "I must have fallen by a double deceit. He must have coloured my innocence with the face of vice, and covered his own notorious vices under the appearance of innocence" *(Works*, VIII, 115). In the *Charge to the Grand Jury* (1749) Fielding eloquently attacks the slanderer, who subverts honor and reputation, for which the best men will undertake the most arduous labors: "Nor is reputation to be considered as a chimerical good, or as merely the food of vanity and ambition. Our worldly interest is closely connected with our fame; by losing this, we are deprived of the chief comforts of society, particularly of that which is most dear to us, the friendship and love of all good and virtuous men" *(Works*, XIII, 217).

11. For the problem of dating the "Essay on the Knowledge of the Characters of Men," see Miller, *Essays on Fielding's Miscellanies*, pp. 189-91.

12. Fielding's last finished work returns to no topic so frequently as the abuse of power by those who have been corrupted by it. One among many acts of inconsiderateness of the captain of the ship provoked the reflection that "I do not, indeed, know so pregnant an instance of the dangerous consequences of absolute power, and its aptness to intoxicate the mind, as that

of those petty tyrants, who become such in a moment, from very well-disposed and social members of that communion, in which they affect no superiority, but live in an orderly state of legal subjection with their fellow-citizens" *(Journal,* p. 65).

II. *Fielding's System of Psychology*

1. George Sherburn, "Fielding's *Amelia:* an Interpretation," in Ronald Paulson, ed., *Fielding* (Englewood Cliffs: Prentice-Hall, 1962), p. 149.

2. *Essays on Fielding's Miscellanies,* p. 215.

3. William Empson, *"Tom Jones,"* in *Fielding,* ed. Paulson, p. 129. Mr. Empson's logic follows the principle that whales and beer kegs are identical because they both have spouts.

4. *Essay Concerning Human Understanding,* II, xx, 14; "Pleasure and pain, and that which causes them, good and evil, are the hinges on which our passions turn" (II, xx, 3).

5. *Fable of the Bees,* I, 39.

6. *Characteristicks,* II, 37-38. "If there be any part of the Temper in which ill Passions or Affections are seated, whilst in another part the Affections towards moral Good are such as absolutely to master those Attempts of their Antagonists; this is the greatest *Proof* imaginable, that a strong Principle of Virtue lies at the bottom, and has possess'd it-self of the natural Temper. Whereas if there be no ill Passions stirring, a Person may be indeed more *cheaply virtuous;* that is to say, he may conform himself to the known Rules of Virtue, without sharing so much of a virtuous Principle as another." All actions by any animal are "done only thro some Affection or Passion, as of Fear, Love, or Hatred moving him. And as it is impossible that a weaker Affection shou'd overcome a stronger, so it is impossible but that where the Affections or Passions are strongest in the main, and form in general the most considerable Party, either by their Force or Number; thither the Animal must incline: and according to this *Ballance* he must be govern'd, and led to Action" (II, 86).

7. The latitudinarian divines were a powerful influence supporting Shaftesbury's system of psychology. As R. S. Crane has argued, their relatively approving attitude toward the passions suited their belief that human nature was basically good: "For most of the divines who were thus helping to set the tone of eighteenth-century humanitarian exhortation, the words 'charity' and 'benevolence' had a double sense, connoting not only the serviceable and philanthropic actions which the good man performs but still more the tender passions and affections which prompt to these actions and constitute their immediate reward." In opposition to the stoics, "The passions, they insisted with Aristotle, are neither good nor evil in themselves; they may, however, be ordered to virtue, and when so ordered they have a possible value, since they and not our weak reason are the forces which make it possible for us to act at all; to wish to eradicate them from our nature is not only a futile but a misguided desire" ("Suggestions Toward a Genealogy of the 'Man of Feeling,' " p. 214). For a first-rate discussion of early eighteenth-century attitudes toward reason and the passions, see Kathleen Williams,

Jonathan Swift and the Age of Compromise (Lawrence: University of Kansas Press, 1959), esp. pp. 19-90.

8. See particularly W. R. Irwin, *The Making of Jonathan Wild*, pp. 42-78; M. C. Battestin, *The Moral Basis of Fielding's Art, passim;* and H. K. Miller, *Essays on Fielding's Miscellanies*, pp. 54-87.

9. *Essay Concerning Human Understanding*, II, xxi, 35.

10. Mandeville stresses man's tendency toward delusive rationalization. All those who claim to be dispassionate, Mandeville says, are merely dormant: "When the Passions lie dormant we have no Apprehension of them, and often People think they have not such a Frailty in their Nature, because that Moment they are not affected with it" *(Fable of the Bees*, I, 139). Categorically, all people who claim to be in love are attempting to satisfy lust, except perhaps the "pale-faced weakly People of cold and phlegmatick Constitutions in either Sex" (I, 144). Even the best people are afraid to look carefully at their own motives.

Shaftesbury was also aware of the power of delusion and was also concerned to suggest ways of avoiding it. For him, however, introspection would not be a depressing experience, since man would find not the devil but merely neutral psychological elements if he saw himself clearly. When the Will is pulled between Appetite and Reason, he says, Reason in time forces Appetite to pay attention, and the next step should be "soliloquy," an examination of the state of the mind: "By this means it will soon happen, that Two form'd *Partys* will erect themselves *within*. For the Imaginations or Fancys being thus roundly treated, are forc'd to declare themselves, and take Party. Those on the side of the elder Brother APPETITE, are strangely subtle and insinuating. They have always the Faculty to speak by Nods and Winks. By this practice they conceal half their meaning . . . till being confronted with their Fellows of a plainer Language and Expression, they are forc'd to quit their mysterious Manner, and discover themselves mere *Sophisters* and *Imposters* who have not the least to do with the Party of REASON and *good Sense*" *(Characteristicks*, I, 188). Domination by the imagination is for Shaftesbury, as it was also for Swift and Locke, the sign of madness (I, 323).

11. In *The Coffee-House Politician* (1730), Justice Worthy is horrified by the ease with which Politic can forget the disappearance of his only daughter when he thinks of the danger of the Turks: "The greatest part of mankind labour under one delirium or other: and Don Quixote differed from the rest, not in madness, but the species of it. The covetous, the prodigal, the superstitious, the libertine, and the coffee-house politician, are all Quixotes in their several ways.

> That man alone from madness free, we find,
> Who, by no wild unruly passion blind,
> To reason gives the conduct of his mind.
>
> *(Works,* IX, 108)

In *The Wedding-Day* (1743), Heartfort wonders why his reason has not overcome his love for the undeserving Charlotte: "had reason the dominion, I should have long expelled the little tyrant, who hath made such ravage there. Of what use is reason then? Why, of the use that a window is to a man in prison, to let him see the horrors he is confined in; but lends him no assistance to his escape" *(Works,* XII, 134).

12. Mr. Miller's analysis of this poem as a key to Fielding's psychology is invaluable: *Essays on Fielding's Miscellanies*, pp. 113-18.

13. For discussion of the Aristotelian (or Horatian) treatment of character in Fielding's novels, see John S. Coolidge, "Fielding and the 'Conservation of Character,'" in *Fielding*, ed. Paulson, pp. 158-76; Homer Goldberg, "Comic Prose Epic or Comic Romance: The Argument of the Preface to *Joseph Andrews*," *PQ*, XLIII (1964), 193-215; Ian Watt, *The Rise of the Novel* (Berkeley & Los Angeles: University of California Press, 1957), pp. 262-80.

14. He is now taking seriously what he had played with in *Jonathan Wild*, a "Machiavellian" program of manipulation; see Bernard Shea, "Machiavelli and Fielding's *Jonathan Wild*," *PMLA*, LXXII (1957), 55-73.

15. George Sherburn, "Fielding's Social Outlook," *PQ*, XXXV (1956), 12, points out that in Fielding's psychological system there is "a sort of duality of the passions" consistent with Sarah Fielding's view, in *The Cry* (1754), that there are two master passions, Love and Pride, and that whichever a man chooses will determine if he is good or bad.

16. In his interesting *Henry Fielding: Mask and Feast* (London: Chatto & Windus, 1965), p. 49, Andrew Wright oddly overstates the implications of this difference from Locke (who was, however, talking of intellect, not disposition): "Fielding's view that human nature is fixed, that character is innate, finds expression in *Amelia* to be sure; to read the first chapter of this novel without appreciating that Fielding owes nothing to Locke for his epistemology is to run the risk of supposing men to be more educable than they really are. To Fielding there is no such thing as a *tabula rasa.* . . ."

III. *Self-enclosure in the Novels*

1. On the romance elements in Fielding's novels, see particularly Sheridan Baker, "The Idea of Romance in the Eighteenth-Century Novel," *PMASAL*, XLIX (1964), 507-22; Sheridan Baker, "Fielding's *Amelia* and the Materials of Romance," *PQ*, XLI (1962), 437-49.

2. In the *Covent-Garden Journal* for January 28, 1752 (I, 186), Fielding says that the *Aeneid* "was the noble model" for *Amelia*. For the parallels, see George Sherburn, "Fielding's *Amelia*: An Interpretation," in *Fielding*, ed. Paulson; Lyall H. Powers, "The Influence of the *Aeneid* on Fielding's *Amelia*," *MLN*, LXXI (1956), 330-36; and Maurice Johnson, *Fielding's Art of Fiction* (Philadelphia: University of Pennsylvania Press, 1961), pp. 139-156.

3. Alan Wendt, in "The Naked Virtue of Amelia," *ELH*, XXVII (1960), 131-148, expands this point to argue that in all of Fielding's novels "the figure of the compelling beautiful and virtuous woman who acts as a Platonic love-object in stimulating men's aspirations" is conspicuous (p. 131).

4. Cf. Marvin Mudrick's discussion, in his *Jane Austen* (Princeton: Princeton University Press, 1952), pp. 95-109, of the simple-complex distinctions in character in *Pride and Prejudice*.

5. The most useful study of Fielding's use of the word "prudence" in *Tom Jones* is Eleanor N. Hutchens, "'Prudence' in *Tom Jones*: A Study of Connotative Irony," *PQ*, XXXIX (1960), 496-507.

6. This interaction between Tom and the other characters has been noted by A. D. McKillop, *The Early Masters of English Fiction* (Lawrence: University of Kansas Press, 1956), p. 121, and by Robert Alter, *Rogue's Progress: Studies in the Picaresque* (Cambridge: Harvard University Press, 1964), pp. 95-96.

7. See especially Battestin, *Moral Basis of Fielding's Art, passim.*

IV. *The Psychology of the Novels*

1. The relative weight to be placed on Adams' virtue and his absurdity is an issue for anyone who takes the novel seriously. Mr. Battestin, concerned with the moral theme, perhaps goes farthest in emphasizing Adams' purity; Stuart M. Tave, in *The Amiable Humorist* (Chicago: University of Chicago Press, 1960), p. 141, is far in the other direction, seeing Adams as confused and vain. Other critics take positions more or less in between.

2. The game of finding the unity of *Joseph Andrews* has been played for over two centuries, beginning with the author's implicit assumption of unity in his Aristotelian discussion of the comic epic in prose in the preface. Elsewhere, Fielding contradicted himself on the kinds of unity to be expected in such a work. In his preface to his sister's *David Simple* (1744), he calls that work a comic prose epic made up of a series of actions, like *Hudibras* in verse or *Don Quixote* in prose, in which "the fable consists of a series of separate adventures, detached from and independent on each other, yet all tending to one great end; so that those who should object want of unity of action here, may, if they please, or if they dare, fly back with their objection in the face even of the Odyssey itself" *(Works,* XVI, 11). But in the *CGJ,* I, 281, he says that one advantage which Charlotte Lennox' *The Female Quixote* has over its model is that "here is a regular Story, which, tho' possibly it is not pursued with that Epic Regularity which would give it the Name of an Action, comes much nearer to that Perfection than the loose unconnected Adventures in Don Quixote; of which you may transverse the Order as you please, without any Injury to the whole." The loose sequence to which he seems to give limited approval is evidently all he had meant by the epic fable in his first novel, and the modern restater of his view, Ethel M. Thornbury, seems on safest ground: see her *Henry Fielding's Theory of the Comic Prose Epic* (Madison: University of Wisconsin Press, 1931), p. 108. M. C. Battestin has argued cogently in *The Moral Basis of Fielding's Art* that the novel is unified by the theme of charity as a contrast to vanity; Maynard Mack, in *"Joseph Andrews* and *Pamela,"* in *Fielding,* ed. Paulson, pp. 52-58, that the polarity of city and country symbols forms a structural unity; Irvin Ehrenpreis, in "Fielding's Use of Fiction: The Anatomy of *Joseph Andrews,"* in *Twelve Original Essays on Great English Novels,* ed. Charles Shapiro (Detroit: Wayne State University Press, 1960), that the novel follows a regular pattern of fits and starts; Maurice Johnson, in *Fielding's Art of Fiction,* p. 49, that the structure follows *Don Quixote's* pattern of contrasting styles; and Andrew Wright, in *Henry Fielding: Mask and Feast,* that individual books of the novel are unified. The scope for further ingenuity seems limited.

3. The squire's huge moral flaws are sometimes slighted these days, when

we are all admirers of ebullient passion. Martin Price, for example, in *To the Palace of Wisdom* (New York: Doubleday, 1964), p. 307, says that Fielding uses Western "to embody animal energy without either the selfish cunning that builds upon appetites in some or the generous charity that fuses with appetite (and transforms it) in others. Tom stands between Western and Allworthy, able to participate in the worlds of both—an innocent carnality in Western and a rational charity in Allworthy—and to bring them together." But Western's innocence is qualified by selfish brutality (as witness his treatment of his wife), and he is not particularly carnal. Fielding was not an admirer of the noble savage; as Andrew Wright notes, he was thoroughly committed to civilization.

4. Ian Watt, in *The Rise of the Novel*, Chapter IX, extensively examines the implications of Fielding's Aristotelian subordination of character to plot. In a beautifully condensed and perceptive study, *Fielding: Tom Jones* (London: Edward Arnold, 1964), Irvin Ehrenpreis suggests, however, that "Fielding does not in fact base the true movement of his work upon what is usually called 'action.' For all the bustle and business of the story the most important happenings, which determine the effective 'plot' can hardly be described as physical deeds. Rather they might be called insights. As in *Clarissa*, the dramatic moments in *Tom Jones* are moments of sudden understanding" (p. 23). But are not moments of sudden understanding also action?

5. In taking up the issue, Fielding involves himself again on the side of the latitudinarians, as Mr. Battestin argued *(Moral Basis of Fielding's Art*, p. 13); to deists like Square stoicism was likely to be a substitute for religion, and to the more severe divines it could be the moral core of Christianity. Bonamy Dobree, *English Literature in the Early Eighteenth Century, 1700-1740* (Oxford: Clarendon Press, 1959), p. 25, attests to its remarkable vitality as one aspect of religion in the period: "L'Estrange's presentation of *Seneca* reached its tenth edition in 1711; Jeremy Collier published his Meditations of Marcus Aurelius in 1700, the first of the fifty-eight editions which appeared during the century."

6. George Sherburn makes this point most cogently in "Fielding's Social Outlook," *PQ*, XXXV (1956), 8.

7. Among the more prominent rivulets in the recent flood of rhetorical studies on Fielding are: Wayne C. Booth, "The Self-Conscious Narrator in Comic Fiction before *Tristram Shandy*," *PMLA*, LXVII (1952), 163-85; Ronald Paulson's Introduction to his edition of modern critical essays, *Fielding*; A. R. Humphreys, "Fielding's Irony: Its Method and Effects," pp. 12-24 of that collection; Wayne C. Booth, *The Rhetoric of Fiction* (Chicago: University of Chicago Press, 1961), which threatens to precipitate reams of further rhetorical studies on everybody; Eleanor N. Hutchens, " 'Prudence' in *Tom Jones*: A Study of Connotative Irony," *PQ*, XXXIX (1960), 496-507; Eleanor N. Hutchens, "Verbal Irony in *Tom Jones*," *PMLA*, LXXVII (1962), 46-50; Eleanor N. Hutchens, *Irony in Tom Jones* (University: University of Alabama Press, 1965); Sheldon Sacks, *Fiction and the Shape of Belief: A Study of Henry Fielding* (Berkeley & Los Angeles: University of California Press, 1964); Andrew Wright, *Henry Fielding: Mask and Feast* (London: Chatto & Windus, 1965).

V. *Environment*

1. In the *Journey from this World to the Next,* the narrator and his com-companions meet a number of souls who are soon to enter the flesh. Two are arm in arm: "one of them was intended for a duke, and the other for a hackney coachman." A prude wonders at this combination, at which they laugh and explain that they "had exchanged lots: for that the duke had with his dukedom drawn a shrew of a wife, and the coachman only a single state" *(Works,* II, 233).

2. Cf. George Sherburn, "Fielding's Social Outlook," *PQ,* XXXV (1956), 2: "Fielding's social 'philosophy' is founded upon the concept of a stratified society, such as might constitute a small section of the great scale of being. He believes that all government is based on a principle of subordination and that the duty of all classes of men is to contribute to the good of the Whole"; Henry Knight Miller, *Essays on Fielding's Miscellanies,* p. 188: "In retrospect, some of Fielding's own values may appear on the 'bourgeois' side. But in a social sense, there is no doubt that his sympathies lay nearer to the values of the aristocratic world—despite his attacks on its excesses—than to the middle-class norms with which he has so often been associated in modern estimates."

3. As for example Charles, Duke of Marlborough, to whom Fielding dedicated *The Universal Gallant* (1735): "Poverty has imposed chains on mankind equal with tyranny; and your Grace has shown as great an eagerness to deliver men from the former, as your illustrious grandfather did to rescue them from the latter" *(Works,* XI, 75).

4. Cf. Justice Squeezum in *The Coffee-House Politician* to a constable who says he has not raided a gambling house because he saw two coaches with coronets at the door: "You did right. The laws are turnpikes, only made to stop people who walk on foot, and not to interrupt those who drive through them in their coaches" *(Works,* IX, 94); the Don, in *Don Quixote in England:* ". . . I tell thee, caitiff, gaols in all countries are only habitations for the poor, not for men of quality. If a poor fellow robs a man of fashion of five shillings, to gaol with him: but the man of fashion may plunder a thousand poor, and stay in his own house" *(Works,* XI, 17); one beau to another (in *Eurydice*) who has joined him in hell and wants the devil to be told that he was hanged, so that he may be well received: "No, hanged, no; then he will take you for a poor rogue, a sort of people he abominates so, that there are scarce any of them here. No, if you would recommend yourself to him, tell him you deserved to be hanged, and was too great for the law" *(Works,* XI, 274).

5. In a *CGJ* essay of August 8, 1752, after reporting the venality of an election meeting, Fielding says he hopes the English will not lose their freedom as the Greeks and Romans had: "I mean by extending it to such an intolerable Degree of Licentiousness, and ungovernable Insolence, as to introduce that Anarchy which is sure to end in some Species of Tyranny or other" (II, 79).

6. "Fielding's Social Outlook," p. 12.

7. In his provocative "Joseph as Hero of *Joseph Andrews,*" *Tulane Studies in English,* VII (1957), 103, Dick Taylor, Jr., argues that the depravity of this squire indicates that Fielding had supported Joseph in the earlier argument. However, Sir Thomas Booby's own triviality, and the various comments elsewhere by Fielding, make such a conclusion questionable.

VI. *Fantasy and Actuality*

1. In *Fielding's Art of Fiction,* Maurice Johnson writes illuminatingly of this characteristic of Fielding's technique, particularly as it appears in *Joseph Andrews.*

2. R. S. Crane, "The Concept of Plot and the Plot of *Tom Jones,*" in *Critics and Criticism,* ed. R. S. Crane (Chicago: University of Chicago Press, 1952), p. 638, significantly pointed out the implications of danger which suffuse the comic actions of the novel.

3. "Life may as properly be called an art as any other; and the great incidents in it are no more to be considered as mere accidents than the several members of a fine statue or a noble poem. The critics in all these are not content with seeing any thing to be great without knowing why and how it came to be so. By examining carefully the several gradations which conduce to bring every model to perfection, we learn truly to know that science in which the model is formed: as histories of this kind, therefore, may properly be called models of HUMAN LIFE, so, by observing minutely the several incidents which tend to the catastrophe or completion of the whole, and the minute causes whence those incidents are produced, we shall best be instructed in this most useful of all arts, which I call the ART OF LIFE" *(Amelia,* I, i).

4. Mr. Battestin, in *The Moral Basis of Fielding's Art,* pp. 30 ff., convincingly places Adams within a contemporary homiletic tradition which made the wanderings of Abraham in exile models of faith and good works; but he tends to minimize the likelihood that at this stage Fielding is using Isaac Barrow for allusive humor, as he elsewhere in the novel uses such favorite authors as Sophocles and Homer.

5. The differences in tone are well worth noting as an indication of Fielding's departure from the traditional distinctions between novel and romance, as Congreve made them in his preface to *Incognita:* "Romances are generally composed of the Constant Loves and invincible Courages of Hero's, Heroins, Kings and Queens, Mortals of the first Rank, and so forth; where lofty Language, miraculous Contingencies and impossible Performances, elevate and surprize the Reader into a giddy Delight. . . . Novels are of a more familiar nature; Come near us, and represent to us Intrigues in practice, delight us with Accidents and odd Events, but not such as are wholly unusual or unpresidented, such which not being so distant from our Belief bring also the pleasure near us. Romances give more of Wonder, Novels more Delight"; respectively, Congreve concludes, they are analogous to tragedy and comedy. *(Incognita,* ed. H. F. B. Brett-Smith, Oxford, Blackwell, 1922, pp. 5-6.) For Fielding, as for Congreve, the romance element allows unreality, but the reality provided by the novel is not only the comedy—it is also the grimness not called for by tradition. Don Quixote's Spain offers few inevitable threats to a gentleman, even an impoverished one; the England of Joseph or Tom or Booth would be deadly without the help of romance.

6. Cf. R. S. Crane, "The Concept of Plot and the Plot of *Tom Jones,*" p. 642: "Both the story told to Tom by the Man of the Hill and that recounted to Sophia by Mrs. Fitzpatrick, however much they owe to the convention of interpolated narratives which Fielding had inherited, along with other devices, from the earlier writers of 'comic romance,' are clearly designed as negative analogies to the moral states of the hearers. . . ."

7. For a vigorous argument to the contrary, see Sheridan Baker, "Fielding's *Amelia* and the Materials of Romance," *PQ*, XLI (1962), 437-49.

8. For an acute discussion of the change in Joseph's character, see Dick Taylor, Jr., "Joseph as Hero of *Joseph Andrews*," *Tulane Studies in English*, VII (1957), 91-109.

9. In *Don Quixote in England* Fielding uses the figure of the Don to indicate a combination of intuitively right moral vision and self-delusion incapable of dealing with the complexities of the world. Similar combinations of qualities as constituents of quixotism occur in *Love in Several Masques* (*Works*, VIII, 83) and *The Coffee-House Politician* (*Works*, IX, 108, 109-10). Stuart M. Tave, *The Amiable Humorist*, pp. 155-57, traces Fielding's use of the ambiguous Quixote figure in the plays.

10. In *Tom Thumb*, the Queen loves Tom, who loves her daughter; in *The Author's Farce*, the hero loves and is beloved by the landlady's daughter, while the landlady wants to marry him. In *Love in Several Masques*, Lady Trap tells Merital: "Ha! I am alone, in the dark, a bedchamber by, if you should attempt my honour, who knows what the frailty of my sex may consent to?" (*Works*, VIII, 59). *Joseph Andrews* is built in the beginning on Joseph's subjection to the lustful attacks of older women of superior station. The second novel also has a hero whose misfortune it is to be immensely attractive to women, but here the myth is brought down to plausibility. All had good reasons besides Tom's beauty: Sophia admired his virtues as well, Molly was eager to profit from his social position and wealth, and both Jenny Waters and Lady Bellaston, as middle-aged women, are in Mrs. Slipslop's condition of lusting after handsome young men generally. In the last novel, though the emphasis is on the sexual perils of Amelia, Booth's adventures with Miss Matthews underlie a good part of the plot.

11. "*Joseph Andrews* and *Pamela*," in *Fielding*, ed. Paulson, pp. 55-56.

12. Lady Booby "entered the parish amidst the ringing of bells, and the acclamations of the poor, who were rejoiced to see their patroness returned after so long an absence, during which time all her rents had been drafted to London, without a shilling being spent among them, which tended not a little to their utter impoverishing; for, if the court would be severely missed in such a city as London, how much more must the absence of a person of great fortune be felt in a little country village, for whose inhabitants such a family finds a constant employment and supply; and with the offals of whose table the infirm, aged, and infant poor are abundantly fed, with a generosity which hath scarce a visible effect on their benefactor's pockets!" (IV, i).

13. See *Love in Several Masques* (*Works*, VIII, 20, 53); *The Temple Beau* (*Works*, VIII, 125); *The Lottery*, which concerns a country girl and a city slicker who fool each other, with the girl finally going to her elegant country-squire pursuer; *The Letter Writers* (*Works*, IX, 163); *The Universal Gallant*, in which Clarinda the country girl is much more honest, fresh, and direct than her town aunts Lady Raffler and Mrs. Raffler; *Pasquin*, which includes a scene of political bribery in a country town, whose mayoress and her daughter are desperate to get to London; and *The Champion* of December 22, 1739 (*Works*, XV, 114), and February 7, 1740 (*Works*, XV, 187). For further discussions of Fielding's views of city and country, see Battestin, *The Moral Basis of Fielding's Art*, p. 92; Miller, *Essays on Fielding's Miscellanies*, p. 127; Wright, *Henry Fielding: Mask and Feast*, p. 85.

VII. Conclusion

1. *The Champion* of January 17, 1740, consists of a discussion of abuse of words (for which Locke is cited as an authority) and lists ways in which they are made meaningless (*Works*, XV, 159); No. 23 of the *True Patriot* attacks shoptalk as an aspect of solipsism, pointing out that various professions or social classes read books and respond to plays along the lines of their own limitations, and that "the divine, the free-thinker, the citizen, the whig, the tory" mean different things by the word "good" (*Works*, XIV, 51); the *CGJ* of January 14, 1752, contains a "Modern Glossary" of the perversion of words like "Knowledge," "Love," "Modesty" in fashionable speech (I, 155-57).

2. For various definitions and derivations of sentimentalism, see, e.g., Lois Whitney, *Primitivism and the Idea of Progress in English Popular Literature of the Eighteenth Century* (Baltimore: Johns Hopkins University Press, 1934), p. 102; Douglas Bush, *Science and English Poetry* (New York: Oxford University Press, 1950), p. 60; Joseph Wood Krutch, *Five Masters* (London: Jonathan Cape, 1931), pp. 160-161; Ernest Dilworth, *The Unsentimental Journey of Laurence Sterne* (New York: King's Crown Press, 1948), *passim*, esp. pp. 6-7; W. F. Galloway, Jr., "The Sentimentalism of Goldsmith," *PMLA*, XLVIII (1933), 1177; Ernest Bernbaum, *The Drama of Sensibility* (Gloucester, Mass.: Peter Smith, 1958, a rpt. of Harvard Studies in English, Vol. III, 1915), p. 10; Arthur Sherbo, *English Sentimental Drama* (East Lansing: Michigan State University Press, 1957), p. 21; Paul E. Parnell, "The Sentimental Mask," *PMLA*, LXXVIII (1963), 529-35.

3. Perhaps the most famous attack on Fielding's morality by a non-Richardsonian contemporary, that of Sir John Hawkins, most clearly presents the objections of the respectable. In his *Life of Samuel Johnson, LL.D.* (London, 1787), he writes of *Tom Jones:* "His morality, in respect that it resolves virtue into good affection, in contradiction to moral obligation and a sense of duty, is that of Lord Shaftesbury vulgarised, and is a system of excellent use in palliating the vices most injurious to society. He was the inventor of the cant-phrase, goodness of heart, which is every day used as a substitute for probity, and means little more than the virtue of a horse or a dog; in short, he has done more towards corrupting the rising generation than any writer we know of " (p. 215). Hawkins' further attack on the novelists, occasioned by a discussion of Richardson, legitimately points up the danger of the morality he describes: "Their generous notions supersede all obligation: they are a law to themselves, and having good hearts and abounding in the milk of human kindness, are above those considerations that bind men to that rule of conduct which is founded in a feeling of duty. Of this new school of morality, Fielding, Rousseau, and Sterne are the principal teachers, and great is the mischief they have done by their documents" (p. 218).

4. See particularly Fielding's discussion of the relative qualities of historians, biographers (i.e., novelists like himself), and romance writers, in *Joseph Andrews,* III, i.

5. In a letter to Mrs. Donnellan of February 22, 1752, Richardson gleefully listed all the parallels for Fielding's characters among Fielding's acquaintances and concluded, "As I said (witness also his hamper plot) he has little or no invention": *Selected Letters of Samuel Richardson,* ed. John Carroll (Oxford: Clarendon Press, 1964), p. 197. But a novelist much different from both surprisingly shared Fielding's views: "Imagination, not invention, is the supreme master of art as of life. An imaginative and exact rendering of au-

thentic memories may serve worthily that spirit of piety towards all things human which sanctions the conceptions of a writer of tales, and the emotions of the man reviewing his own experience": Joseph Conrad, *A Personal Record*, in *The Mirror of the Sea and A Personal Record*, ed. M. D. Zabel (New York: Doubleday Anchor Books, 1960), p. 213.

6. Fielding's preface to his sister's *David Simple* had anticipated this view: "the merit of this work consists in a vast penetration into human nature, a deep and profound discernment of all the mazes, windings, and labyrinths, which perplex the heart of man to such a degree that he is himself often incapable of seeing through them; and . . . this is the greatest, noblest, and rarest, of all the talents which constitute a genius . . ." (*Works*, XVI, 10).

7. Such a view of invention is not original with Fielding, going back to classical theory (in Horace particularly) and widespread in the eighteenth century. The preface to Pope's *Iliad*, for example, says of Homer that "If we observe *Descriptions, Images,* and *Similes,* we shall find the Invention still predominant. To what else can we ascribe that vast Comprehension of Images of every sort, where we see each Circumstance and Individual of Nature summon'd together by the Extent and Fecundity of his Imagination; to which all things, in their various Views, presented themselves in an Instant, and had their Impressions taken off to Perfection at a Heat?": "Preface to . . . *Iliad*," in *Critical Essays of the Eighteenth Century, 1700-1725*, ed. Willard Higley Durham (New Haven: Yale University Press, 1915), p. 331; see Walter Jackson Bate, *From Classic to Romantic* (Cambridge: Harvard University Press, 1946), p. 10, and Louis Bredvold, "The Tendency toward Platonism in Neo-Classical Esthetics," *ELH*, I (1934), 91-120, for illuminating discussions of the idea of nature in the aesthetic theory of the eighteenth century.

Index